The Future of
the Christian World Mission

The Future of the Christian World Mission

Studies in Honor of R. Pierce Beaver

edited by
William J. Danker
Wi Jo Kang

WILLIAM B. EERDMANS PUBLISHING COMPANY
Grand Rapids, Michigan

Table of Contents

Preface

As an historian Professor R. Pierce Beaver is concerned with the past, but as a professor of missions he is profoundly oriented to the future. Trained in the highest traditions of his discipline, he surveys the past and the present of world mission with critical objectivity and sober realism, and he sees the world mission of tomorrow standing in mortal danger because of mounting apathy and neo-isolationism. As few others, he recognizes how tragically ironic it is that many supporters who shared the toil of sowing and cultivation should be deserting the mission in the very hour of an often astonishing harvest. He understands from personal observation the dimensions of the existing worldwide Christian church that is the monument and vindication of the pioneers he has studied so well. He sees by faith the outlines of a world church in the next generation, whose adherents in the Third World may outnumber Christians in the Atlantic community, the historic base of the mission.

It was Professor Gerald Anderson, then of Union Theological Seminary, near Manila, who suggested the idea of a festschrift to one of the editors. And the other editor confided that he himself had been nurturing such a plan. And thus, appropriately, a happy Asian-American coeditorship came into being. Both editors studied under Professor Beaver, one completing his dissertation under his guidance, the other recommended by Beaver to Professor Hans-Werner Gensichen at Heidelberg. Thanks to such thoughtful kindness, one of the undersigned had the privilege of studying not only under the dean of professors of mission in North America but also under an outstanding European missiologist.

The contributors to this book were chosen with little regard for confessional affiliation. But due to the problems that have overtaken all religious publishing, especially of mission litera-

ture, this study is not as inclusive as we would like. In the interest of the wide circulation a Beaver festschrift deserves, we
fought off our inclination to produce a large and costly volume.
Regrettably, therefore, many distinguished names in all parts of
the world could not be represented. Yet, our contributors have
touched on virtually every vital concern in the Christian world
mission today. In the lead-off essay W. Richey Hogg provides
an astronaut's view, as it were, of the *oikoumene*, the whole in-
habited earth. His first projection suggests that the world mission in the next thirty years may be more nearly like that in the
third century than in the nineteenth, and that it stands on the
threshold of a dramatic advance. Dr. Hogg is basically optimistic. Christianity's "faithful remnants" within the nominal billion adherents of the church, reside in almost every nation on
earth, display remarkable vitality, and steadily generate dynamic
new Christian movements. In spite of divisions, Christians increasingly dedicate themselves to life together for the world.

Hans-Werner Gensichen analyzes the mutual shock which
Christianity and the non-Christian religions experience in their
close and continuous encounter within the world village whose
inhabitants share a common history. He reviews four models for
dialogue between the two — addition, reduction, evolution, and
absolutism — and rejects them in favor of a dialogue based on
"solidarity" and "witness."

Kosuke Koyama views the future of the Christian world mission in the double historical perspective of "gun" and "ointment." Though it is specifically Asia that he views through these
intriguing twin prisms, the incongruity of "gun" and "ointment"
applies as well to the West's contacts with the entire non-Western world.

Lothar Schreiner will delight the heart of Professor Beaver
and every other historically minded reader as he shares a previously unpublished manuscript describing the early missionary
exploration of British Baptists among the Toba Bataks in 1824.
This will be new to the many readers who have supposed that
the first missionaries to venture into Batak country were Henry
Lyman and Samuel Munson of the American Board of Commissioners for Foreign Missions, who were killed by the Bataks in
1834. Schreiner concludes by outlining the present challenges
faced by the Batak Church, now a million members strong.

Prudencio Damboriena puts his missiological expertise and wide experience as a missionary in Latin America and Asia into a disarmingly candid description of the present missionary crisis in Roman Catholicism. He comes to serious grips with Karl Rahner's concept of "anonymous Christianity," and goes on to challenge Rahner's disciples, who see the non-Christian religions as "ordinary" ways of salvation, while the church is regarded as the "extraordinary" means.

Harold Lindsell is equally candid as he forthrightly witnesses to the position of evangelicals and describes their present condition. While calling attention to certain hopeful developments, his general assessment of the world mission among evangelical churches is not an optimistic one.

Arthur F. Glasser offers a somewhat more optimistic picture. While acknowledging that the evangelical mission faces many serious difficulties, Professor Glasser is greatly encouraged by the revivals occurring among students and by what he discerns as a "new mood of evangelism currently upon the worldwide Protestant church," a mood that has resulted in many new and creative missionary programs and structures.

Representing those countless students whom Pierce Beaver so profoundly influenced in their pastoral outlook is F. Dean Lueking. After writing his doctoral dissertation under Professor Beaver, he became minister of a large church in one of Chicago's near suburbs. Fittingly, his essay concretizes the mission through which God seeks people in redeeming love. He describes three people. The first is a youth with shoulder-length red hair who seeks an inner life. The second is a disaffected millionaire woman who no longer comes to church or gives anything at all because she is upset about the church's concern for social issues. She symbolizes the need for patient pastoral work to overcome the growing polarization of left and right in the churches of the Atlantic community. The third person is a seventeen-year-old black youth who finds new hope in something called the Black Diaconate.

With a remarkable record of scholarly editorial work in missions assembled while active at a seminary on the mission frontier, Gerald Anderson reports comprehensively on research, writing and publishing about the Christian world mission. He pays special tribute to R. Pierce Beaver and the "Christian

World Mission Books" Beaver is editing for Eerdmans. While pessimistic about many aspects of religious publishing in general and mission publishing in particular, Anderson points out the need for missiologists who will "clarify and define for a confused and lukewarm church the meaning of mission in an age which is both ecumenical and secular," as Pierce Beaver himself pointed out in his 1968 address at the first Anglo-European consultation on mission studies at Selly Oak Colleges, Birmingham. In addition to asking for many other needed studies, Anderson describes available research resources. This essay provides an invaluable compact tool for mission scholars.

James A. Scherer writes of the future of "Missions in Theological Education" on the basis of an historical retrospect. He notes that missiology must be distinguished by versatility, adaptability, and readiness for humble service. While theology tends to view itself arrogantly as the focus of the church, a versatile and adaptable missiology must graciously remind theologians that the purpose of theology is the mission of God.

In "A Piece of the Action" one of the editors reports on the new economic base many Asian churches are establishing in their ministry to the modern vertical dimension of the urban world.

The other editor, drawing on his Oriental heritage of profound respect for the rare teacher who becomes one's own personal mentor, writes a biographical tribute to Professor Beaver that will reflect the sentiments of many who studied under him, worked with him, and knew him in the Christian world mission.

We are bold enough to trust that our contributors have provided a book both comprehensive and penetrating. Christian leaders in world mission on all six continents will find it illuminating. Friends — and critics — of the world mission will find it revealing and honest. We hope pastors will read it and commend it to lay people. We dare to hope that study groups ranging all the way from local churches to university and divinity-school classes will hit upon the idea of considering this festschrift for a textbook. There could be no finer way for many people to participate in honoring a distinguished scholar who is above all a mission educator. Every blow against indifference to world mission and the ignorance and misinformation it feeds upon would warm his heart. Nothing would please him more than to have this volume read not only by other mission scholars but by persons of many varied backgrounds.

We present this festschrift as a modest token of the esteem in which Professor R. Pierce Beaver is held by the Christian world mission and, therefore, by the world church.

—WI JO KANG

— WILLIAM J. DANKER

W. RICHEY HOGG, a minister of the United Methodist Church, is Professor of World Christianity at Perkins School of Theology, Southern Methodist University, Dallas, Texas. From 1950 to 1952 he was an Executive Assistant in the New York office of the International Missionary Council. From 1952 to 1955 he was a missionary in India, serving as Professor of Church History in Leonard Theological College, Jabalpur, India. He did his undergraduate work at Duke University and completed his seminary training at Yale University, where he also received a Ph.D. in 1951. With K. S. Latourette he wrote *Tomorrow Is Here.* He is also the author of *Ecumenical Foundations* and *One World — One Mission,* and is one of the editors of the three-volume *History of American Methodism.*

1

W. Richey Hogg: The Oikoumene

Men look increasingly toward the year 2000 A.D. Gateway to a new century and a new millennium, that date — only thirty years away — exerts tremendous fascination. As that year approaches, how will the world mission manifest itself in and through the Ecumenical Movement? It is to this question that I wish to address myself in this article.

The Ecumenical Era. Man has entered and is irrevocably committed to the ecumenical era — in science, politics, business, economics, and religion. The oneness of mankind on this planet is now inescapable. That is the view from outer space. Communications satellites, space capsules that girdle the earth in ninety minutes, and the ever-present threat of mushroom clouds spilling their lethal fallout for years to come on all mankind confirm this.

Other equally significant evidences are mounting. The central banks of the world's major non-Communist nations have for more than a decade worked in closest alliance because the interacting, interdependent world community requires this. Giant global corporations no longer structure themselves as national companies with international outreach. They now emerge as multi-national concerns with major bases in two or three nations and with lesser bases scattered throughout the world. Perhaps the prime symbol of the world's physical oneness is the United Nations — and its weaknesses reveal only too well man's unreadiness for the global community into which he has been thrust.

The Biblical Witness. All this underscores the biblical witness

13

to mankind's unity in creation. It makes urgent the task of God's covenant people to demonstrate that unity — a unity made strong in its diversity. The covenant election at Sinai points not to Israel as God's especially favored people but beyond Israel to all nations. For them Israel was entrusted with a special task. So too, the new covenant in Christ points not to the church as God's most esteemed society among men but beyond it to all mankind. God created the church and gave it its marching orders (its apostolate) for the sake of the whole world of man, the *oikoumene*. The tree of life that stands in the Garden of Eden (Gen. 2:9) appears also in the final chapter of Scripture (Rev. 22:2). That tree emphasizes the great biblical theme of mankind's oneness and of covenant witness to that unity throughout all the world as testimony to the power of God's love. Its leaves are for the healing (salvation) of the nations.

The world mission of God's covenant people produces unity across all the traditional barriers of race and nation that divide men. In turn, this very unity becomes the validating power of that mission, which declares God's holy love and his presence and work in the history of all men. Thus are the world mission and the Ecumenical Movement intertwined.

The Ecumenical Movement. What is the Ecumenical Movement? Eluding neat definition, that movement is best explained by describing some of its many and diverse elements. These include the worldwide network of church councils that has emerged in the past sixty-three years. Americans are familiar with councils of churches at the city, state, and national level. But beyond this, around the globe more than seventy national councils are at work, and within the past thirteen years regional councils have begun operating in Asia, Africa, Europe, and the Pacific. Constituted in 1948, the World Council of Churches (WCC) is the most formidable in membership and outreach.

The Ecumenical Movement also embraces all that has emerged from Vatican II. It includes the more than fifty church unions in the past five decades, among them the United Church of Canada in 1925, Japan's *Kyodan*, which evolved fully after World War II, the Church of South India in 1947, and the Church of North India, constituted in 1970. It also includes the growing momentum toward union. More than forty specific union negotiations are now in progress. It is reflected in the growing sense of unity within the entire world Christian community and in the myriad unheralded local instances of love, unity, and renewal that give substance to the whole. In all this, the eye of faith discerns the remarkable work of the Holy Spirit leading the church to a fuller unity for the sake of the world.

Yet in early June, 1910, before the World Missionary Conference met at Edinburgh, who would have dared to project such developments within sixty years? Except for one body in the U.S.A., none of the organized evidences of the Ecumenical Movement here mentioned then existed. For that matter, in the summer of 1958 — six months before Pope John's announcement — who could have foreseen Vatican II or known that this Council with its ever-widening impact would become the dominant ecumenical fact of the sixties? Those two indications alone suggest the problem of trying to read the ecumenical future.

I. PARALLELS WITH THE THIRD CENTURY

Indications today suggest that the mission throughout the *oikoumene* in the next generation may be more like that in the third century than like that in the nineteenth. In short, the old European Christendom, with its close alliance of church and state and the decisive shaping of culture resulting from it, is dead. The first century of the post-Constantinian (or post-Christendom) age is underway.

The Church in the Third Century. By 313 A.D. Constantine was rising to power. A few years before this in the Mediterranean world, Christians constituted a majority of the population only in several small areas and in a few cities. In many cities they represented a substantial minority, but elsewhere they constituted only a tiny segment of the population. Of the Roman Empire's probably 50 million people, Christians numbered about 5 million. A 10-per-cent minority, they were well dispersed. That age knew widespread religious hunger, and Christians lived amidst a welter of competing religions and systems of faith. To assure minimal religious uniformity, citizens were required to acknowledge the emperor as divine. This was a trifling obligation for most citizens, but Christians refused. And as members of an illegal movement, they knew persecution — some of it subtle, much of it savage. Intellectuals judged them

15

ignorant, and mobs shouted their derision. But most of society ignored them.

The inner dynamic and outward thrust of this committed, interracial, international minority had its impact, however. For while the early church was certainly far from perfect, the decisive picture it presented to the world was that of a diverse, but united, supportive, and caring community. Many noted the informal but effective lines of inter-church aid, even across the Mediterranean, and they saw also that Christians, when they could, helped non-Christians. Despite all that beset them, these people obviously believed they were serving God's purpose for the world. And for increasing numbers their faith became "the way."

The Post-Constantinian Era. Moving toward the twenty-first century, Christians in the post-Constantinian era of today are finding many similarities with the third century. For example, while in Europe, North America, South America, and some other areas they represent a majority, they are only a large minority in sub-Saharan Africa, and a tiny minority in Asia. Among the world's 3 billion people they stand nominally as one-third of mankind — only a substantial minority.[1]

Again, despite their divisions but with their rich diversity, Christians throughout the *oikoumene* and across all the traditional barriers of mankind are producing and experiencing growing unity. Yet throughout the world they know persecution. Many are refugees. In a few areas they are outlawed. But usually they confront more subtle social or political suppression. They live amid the whole concourse of man's religions — traditional and modern. In a manner unprecedented since the third century, they are entering into dynamic engagement with all these faiths. That mode of mission is likely to increase. In man's quest for meaning, for certainty, for supportive community, for justice, and for fulfillment, the age demonstrates its deep religious hunger. This is nowhere more evident than in the West — the old Christendom.

The parallels are evident, but there are at least three differ-

---

[1] One may question the meaning of this huge nominal figure for Christians. But in so doing, he must also assess the meaning of "nominal adherents" for other religions. For example, what does it mean to say that Hindus and Muslims comprise 30 per cent of mankind?

ences that perhaps should be noted. First, the world today is under no single political empire. Instead its whole life is dominated by Western technology, a force separable from the Christian tradition but derived from it. Second, the whole world has moved into an era of universal history. The dynamics of that history — with its view of man and its concern for his rights and material betterment — spring from the Christian faith. Third, Christians have covered the earth, and their faith is rooted among every people. How one evaluates the "true size" of the Christian minority is of little consequence. What is important is that it has achieved a representative spread and influence among mankind unprecedented in human history.

II. EXTENSION OF PRESENT ECUMENICAL PATTERNS

Christianity's "faithful remnants," the committed minority within the larger minority, reside among almost every people on earth, display remarkable vitality, and are steadily generating dynamic new Christian movements. Within that milieu, much that is already familiarly "ecumenical" will continue to develop.

Church Unions. The growing trend toward church unions is likely to accelerate. In the major twentieth-century trans-confessional unions consummated before 1970, Anglicans were involved in only one — the Church of South India. Of the union negotiations now underway, a majority include Anglicans. Two considerations immediately appear. First, Anglican bodies around the world will increasingly enter united churches, and the Anglican world community will progressively disappear. The same process, of course, can be seen and will be seen among Methodists, Presbyterians, and others.

The second consideration is perhaps more important. The issue of the ministry and the historic episcopate will come sharply to the fore. A major question arises: Will the historic episcopate as *traditionally* understood prevail? Or will a view like that of the Church of South India obtain? Long conversations with the Lutherans have led that church to declare what it has understood implicitly from the beginning: the historic episcopate is useful, but does not require a particular theological interpretation and is not of the *esse* of the church. More than 87 per cent of the world's Protestants (Anglicans included) confirm this belief. If God has been at work in the Protestant tradi-

17

tion and if the living truth of that tradition is also to be appropriated, the decisive importance of the answer given becomes evident. It will help to shape the future of the mission.

Moreover, it takes little imagination to project a rather new development in the near future. For example, should the United Church of Australia come into being, a proposal by its members — none of whom had had episcopacy — that its new bishops be consecrated by those from the Church of South India and that it negotiate full communion with that body would surely be honored. Then one could begin to visualize the growth in Asia of a whole network of national united churches in full communion with one another. Among others, it would include those in North and South India, Pakistan, Ceylon, Malaysia, Australia, and perhaps also in Japan, the Philippines, and elsewhere. That would provide Asia with a new witness to the faith. In turn, the emerging national or regional united churches in Africa, including those in Ghana, Nigeria, Zambia, and East Africa, could well come into full communion with those churches of Asia.

This new community could extend even further. Churches in Britain look expectantly toward union in 1980. The United Church of Canada is conversing with the Anglican Communion. In the United States ten denominations with 25 million members have completed their first decade of negotiation in the Consultation on Church Union (COCU) and look toward a decisive march into union within the next decade. The result, on a global scale, would be a world community of united churches from many nations, not unlike the commonwealth of unity among the Orthodox Churches.

Precisely how such a development, even with many Protestant churches continuing on their own way, would influence the world mission is difficult to say, but I believe that it could be a strongly positive force.

What are the key norms for assessing such unions? One is their ability to overcome cultural, national, caste, and racial separations. These — not denominations — are the fundamental divisions undercutting mission. Another is their power to maintain strong spiritual life in a united community while engaged in relevant social witness. A third is their determination to provide for flexible and varied forms of mission and ministry, of

18

worship and structure as required by the amazing diversity of mankind. A fourth is their commitment and effort to fulfill God's mission in the widest arena open to them.

Recognition of Lay Witness. Lay ecumenical concern and action in and beyond the church should grow. The place and importance of God's people as the agents of his mission is underscored in Vatican II's "Constitution on the Church," in the Church of South India's recent adjustment of its constitution, and in what Christian men and women on every continent are doing. The worldwide decline in the number of men entering the priesthood in the Roman Catholic Church also points to an expanding role in that body for the laity, with its consequent impact on mission.

As many Christians discover their mission "outside" the church in common endeavors to achieve justice and to meet human need, a polarization already evident will grow. This fundamental division cuts across almost all denominations and involves two groups. The first emphasizes the prophetic and active role of the church in society. Its theological justification centers upon God's holy will and his lordship over history. Its practical danger in the drive to humanize man and society is finally to reject any need for the Christian tradition and the gospel. The second focuses upon the priestly role that provides nurture and solace for individuals. Its theological justification is the holy and loving concern of God for the ultimate destiny of each of his children. The practical danger in this effort to convert men and nurture their faith in close community is finally to reject the gospel's demand for the unity of the church and the church's servant-identity with the world.

Democracy demonstrates its strength by holding freedom and equality together in dynamic tension. The church discloses its strength by maintaining in supportive tension its prophetic social role and its priestly personal task. The attempt to achieve this balance will compel the church to search anew for the biblical foundations of its mission. The result, if successful, may be creative; but if unsuccessful, it may be freshly divisive. Roman Catholics and Protestants, sometimes in unusual combination, are caught up together in this.

Bible Translation and Distribution. Cooperation is growing between the Roman Catholic Church and the United Bible

Societies (UBS) in the translation, production, and distribution of the scriptures. Explored and developed in 1967 at the regional conferences for Africa, Asia-Pacific, and Europe, the basic plans found fullest expression at the UBS Regional Conference of the Americas held in Mexico late in 1968. With major focus upon Latin America, where Catholic-Evangelical relations have been most strained, and with reports of noteworthy Catholic-Protestant cooperation there in the production and distribution of the scriptures, that gathering at Oaxtepec gave impetus to the new cooperation. The Vatican Department of Common Bible Word is operating closely with the UBS. "Guiding Principles for Interconfessional Cooperation in Translating the Bible," a statement prepared and released jointly in June, 1968, by the Roman Catholic Secretariat for Promoting Christian Unity and by the UBS, has proved to be a foundation document. In several countries Catholics and Protestants have already agreed to use a commonly acceptable Bible. That trend should accelerate.

Councils of Churches. Councils of churches represent a twentieth-century development. They have appeared locally and nationally where denominations have flourished, as in the United States with its quite different configuration from the European national pattern of one large state church and several small sects. They have demonstrated that denominations cannot alone provide the world with the full ministry or mission of the church.

Councils seem destined to continue. Yet several forces will lead to their being rethought and reshaped. The larger church unions now on the horizon will make a considerable difference. Increasing Roman Catholic willingness to enter cooperative endeavors may call for structural changes. Budgetary considerations and creatively changing roles will be factors. Underlying all these at the deepest level is the question of God's mission and its most responsible fulfillment by the churches together.

The East Asia Christian Conference planning for mission within the triangle marked by Tokyo, Karachi, and Melbourne, the All Africa Church Conference, and other recently constituted regional councils should grow in importance. Often they provide for local bodies or national agencies the nearest and best operating instrument and symbol of Christianity's transnational outreach and community. Significantly, in the first days of Vatican II when all the bishops of Africa were in Rome and together could view their common problems, they formed the Secretariat of the Pan African Episcopate. The Latin American Bishops Council (CELAM), operating with its secretariat, commissions, annual meetings, and occasional large assemblies — the latest at Medellin, Colombia in 1968 — offers a prime example of a regional council with a generative and shaping influence for mission over a vast area.

The Third World. The church in the Third World will come to the fore and occupy a more important place than ever before. By the year 2000, this continuing, decisive shift in Christianity's bases for creative theology, action, and outreach will make it increasingly difficult for the *oikoumene* to regard Christianity as Western.

Ibero-America holds nearly 39 per cent of the world's Roman Catholics, and by the year 2000 the proportion is likely to be more than 50 per cent. The expanding impact there of Vatican II in molding the understanding of church and mission and in channeling that region's revolutionary thrust will be of utmost importance. Priests there are few. Key leaders see the church's great hope ahead in its committed lay forces.

The Roman Catholic Church has been present in Africa for a relatively short time, but its 30 million members there already match those — if one excludes the Philippines, a special case — in all Asia, where its missionaries have been present in strength for more than 450 years. It is concentrating its overseas missionaries in Africa and should find its greatest percentage of growth on this continent. The Orthodox churches, too, will fulfill their overseas mission chiefly in Africa.

Similarly, Protestant bodies will find their greatest growth in Latin America and Africa. Indeed, if present trends continue, Christians by the year 2000 may well constitute a majority in Africa's sub-Saharan population. As for Asia, the 80 million Christians there represent only about 3 per cent of the population. Yet from them may come some of the most creative church unions and the most advanced theological thinking in the Third World. The enlarged role of the churches in Asia, Africa, and Latin America, with their zeal and innovative contributions in liturgy, theology, and life-styles, suggests that the Christian ecumenical community in common cause will be drawing upon the rich diversity of all mankind's resources in a manner new in human history.

The tides now sweeping across the Third World indicate that two great forces will help shape the expression of Christian faith there. First, the masses of Latin America are pushing toward the achievement of justice and human dignity in a new social order. Through the lens of God's purpose for man in history, they will increasingly see their expression of Christian faith as a prophetic calling. Second, the Third World will continue to be in massive encounter with contending faith systems: Latin America with Marxism, Africa with Islam and a receding traditional religion, and Asia with the historic religions as well as the newer faiths. The resulting response will include increasing efforts at witness, several distinct forms of Christian apologia, and dialogue in every form and at every level.

As these realities in the world Christian community come into sharp focus, they will call for a highly sensitized understanding among Western churches, new patterns and kinds of supportive cooperation, and new willingness to learn from others the larger dimensions of Christian faith. The one mission in the whole world will become unmistakably clear.

III. ON THE ECUMENICAL FRONTIERS

Some of the ecumenical engagements that will help to form the nature and pattern of mission in the future will be different from those of the past.

The Evangelicals. Those bodies most closely connected to the recent past designate themselves as "Evangelical" or hold closely allied positions. The three largest of these in the United States number more than 16 million members. A host of smaller denominations of similar inclination would probably add another 14 million. Their combined outreach in world mission is very large. Indeed, with but few exceptions these denominations directly and also through independent and faith missions send far more missionaries overseas than do the cooperating bodies of Protestantism in the United States.

By sheer volume and impact, the work of such groups as the Southern Baptists, the Sudan Interior Mission, and the Wycliffe

Bible Translators — the latter two are faith missions — must be reckoned as of major importance. Yet almost all these bodies share a fundamental fear and mistrust of the Ecumenical Movement. This is compounded variously of the belief that its goal is a monolithic (and thus repressive) church, that this involves eventually a union with the Roman Catholic Church, that its theology is not biblical, and that this aberration leads to unjustified social and political involvement. Over the years, concerned people from both sides have sought to bridge that chasm. For a few individuals those efforts have produced bridges of understanding. But at present this division among Protestant forces shows little promise of resolution.

Pentecostalism. Within world Christianity, Pentecostalism is gaining strength, and nowhere is its magnetism, transforming power, and burgeoning force better seen than in Latin America. Strongest in Brazil and Chile, but also spreading rapidly elsewhere, it makes a deep appeal, changes lives, and produces men for the ministry. These highly visible results evoke amazed and wistful admiration from those who observe, not least from Roman Catholics. So vigorously has it grown in some areas that for many Pentecostalism *is* Protestantism!

In 1961 two Chilean Pentecostal bodies joined the WCC, and in 1969 a large group in Brazil, widely associated with the name of its leader, Manuel de Melo, entered that council. Meanwhile, interest in the WCC mounts among Latin American Pentecostals. They are seeking broader contact and in certain instances are encouraging some theological training for their ministers. These trends suggest sharing and growth with significance for world mission.

African Churches. Many regard the United States as the prime example of a land in which denominational or sectarian division has run rampant. Yet top honor for this dubious distinction belongs to Africa. There, thousands of sects have arisen. They reflect the charismatic appeal of a leader, the sway of intense Africanism, or the power of tribalism. Some advance a genuinely Christian faith. Others incorporate so much traditional African religion that Christian elements are mere traces. Most fall between these two types, but all are staunchly African.

The sectarian atomization of Christian faith and fellowship in Africa appalls many. Yet the African sects have spread the

23

gospel. Accordingly, their fraternal relationships must be handled with Christian insight and love. The full significance of the entry into the WCC[2] in 1969 of the vigorous and widely-representative Kimbanguist Church of the Congo remains to be seen. It may well point toward a growing understanding and sense of community that could direct the course of African Christianity in the future.

Secular Ecumenism. Another new force on the contemporary scene is "secular ecumenism." That phrase frightens some. But the conviction of those who advocate it is rooted in the doctrine of creation, with its emphasis upon God's total sovereignty and his concern for all the world and its people. They advocate cooperation not only among all Christians but also, where possible, with non-Christians in the quest for humane life and justice. Thus John XXIII's *Pacem in Terris* and Paul VII's *Ecclesiam Suam* were addressed to "all men of good will," and Vatican II's "Pastoral Constitution on the Church in the Modern World" was addressed "to all humanity." That Council's "Decree on Ecumenism" declares that "all men without exception are summoned to united effort" (II:12) in a common march toward justice for mankind. The documents of the World Council of Churches reflect similar concern.

Some believe that secular ecumenism, the effort to make common cause with all men, is the goal of Christian mission. Far more view it as only one part of the mission's total task. In fact, many see this concern as secondary, a matter for personal response resulting from mission's primary aim, the conversion of individuals. Some believe it has no place at all in the Christian mission. These divisions, as noted earlier, run deep.

The Underground Church. Somewhat related in its outlook and in the strength of its conviction is the Underground Church. This movement, already worldwide, is strongest in Europe and North America. Most of its members are Roman Catholics, but many non-Roman Christians share in it. Its adherents see many institutional structures of today as irrelevant. They believe that

---

[2] "The World Council of Churches is a fellowship of churches which confess the Lord Jesus Christ as God and Saviour according to the Scriptures and therefore seek to fulfill together their common calling to the glory of the one God, Father, Son and Holy Spirit" (WCC *Constitution,* Art. I, Basis).

"the people of God" constitute the church and must explore new forms of worshipping and witnessing. They hold that the traditional norms of authority for the Christian are subject to the Christian's conscience. Although lacking precise parallels, this drive for renewal, relevance, and outreach reflects many similar movements in Christian history. Its development and meaning probably hinge on the outcome of the present "crisis of authority" in the Roman Catholic Church.

Encounter with Other Religions. This age of deep religious hunger is witnessing the decay of traditional religions and the rapid sweep of new religions — materialism, scientism, nationalism, and others — around the world. Christians everywhere face this challenge — to an extent unparalleled since the second and third centuries. Already well underway, it is far more advanced than most realize. Around the globe it appears on university campuses, in factories, among intellectuals.

Justin Martyr argued that whatever truth there is in other religions is born of God's "generative Word" *(logos spermatikos),* which enlightens every man. This, of course, became overwhelmingly the view of the early church, the result being its wholesale appropriation of Platonic and Aristotelian thought as vehicles for Christian truth. Many Christians today tend to share this attitude. The "Declaration on the Relationship of the Church to Non-Christian Religions" from Vatican II indicates a new Roman Catholic openness to "dialogue and collaboration" (par. 2) with those of other faiths. An intriguing example of this openness in practice is provided by that remarkable Indo-European Fr. Raymond Pannikar, who with his Spanish-Catholic and Indian-Hindu background has tried to establish a role for Hindu philosophy in a Christian theology for the whole *oikoumene.*

IV. THE FUNDAMENTAL QUESTIONS

Today's instant global communication and world travel by students, housewives, and businessmen mean a rapid acceleration of the world's history. Who dares to set limits on what may appear in the next three decades?

As the twenty-first century approaches, the Christian world mission will find its outworking through the Ecumenical Move-

ment, in its broadest sense, in accord with the answers given
to these questions:

1. What is the nature and purpose of God's mission? How
   is it to be fulfilled in the life, witness, and outreach of
   the covenanted community formed and made one in
   Christ?
2. When men of every culture, language, and nation acknowledge Jesus Christ, what is the distinctive nature
   of Christian community?
3. Within the world Christian community what becomes
   the authority for faith and life — the Holy Spirit, the
   Bible, the "Great Tradition" or even *a* tradition, the
   Pope, the individual or the community conscience, or
   some other norm?
4. The fourth underlies the others. God as Creator is at
   work in all his creation and among all men ("Blessed
   be ... Assyria the work of my hands" but also "the rod
   of my anger" — Isaiah 19:25; 10:5), but he has also
   formed his covenanted people in Christ and given them
   to the world. What then is their relation to all men in
   fulfillment of their covenant task? In short, what is the
   relation of the history of salvation to the universal history of the whole *oikoumene?*

The covenant people of God find their life and strength in
one abiding conviction: God, the father of Jesus Christ, is stead-
fastly faithful in his holy love and will bring to triumphant com-
pletion his purpose intended in creation for history. Given to
the world as its suffering servants, they contribute life amid
perplexing problems, not neatly packaged certainties. In the
next generation, the human translation of God's mission into
life together for God's world will be a key determinant in shaping the Christian world mission.

HANS-WERNER GENSICHEN is Professor of the History of Religions and Missiology at Heidelberg University, Germany. From 1952 to 1957 he served as Professor of Church History at the Tamil Evangelical Lutheran Church Divinity School in Tranquebar and at Gurukul Lutheran Theological College in Madras, India. He was Africa secretary of the Theological Education Fund from 1961 to 1964. He studied at the universities of Leipzig, Königsberg, Tübingen, and Göttingen and at Princeton Theological Seminary. He received his Th.D. from Göttingen University, his Th.D. h.c. from Hamburg University. He is the chairman of Deutsche Gesellschaft für Missionswissenschaft, co-editor of *Evangelische Missions-Zeitschrift* and *Theologische Stimmen aus Asien, Afrika und Latein-amerika,* and author of *Das Taufproblem in der Mission, Die Kirche von Südindien, Missionsgeschichte der neueren Zeit, Living Mission,* and other publications.

2

Hans-Werner Gensichen: Dialogue with Non-Christian Religions

I

THE STATE OF AFFAIRS IS NOW QUITE DIFFERENT FROM EITHER A century ago or a decade past. It is just as hostile to an easy expansion of the Christian faith as the world climate of that time was favourable to it."[1] This diagnosis of the prospects for Christian mission is as valid today as it was when R. Pierce Beaver offered it to an Indian audience thirteen years ago. The alternative has since become even more inescapable. Christianity may under the pressures of time and change decide to "refuse acknowledgment of the continuing there-ness of diverse faiths"[2] and concentrate on its own parochial well-being. But that would be tantamount to what Paul called "going out of the world" and renouncing the essential sent-ness of the faith. If that option is declined, as it must be, and if Christianity is to aim at more than mere survival, as it should, it must honestly meet the new challenges of a non-Christian world, without abandoning its loyalty to Christ.

It is essential to understand the deep changes which determine the present situation and will most certainly determine the future as well. They have been aptly described as a wave of shocks to the very foundations of all religions, producing unpredictable results. As far as Christianity is concerned, there is,

---

[1] *The Christian World Mission* (Calcutta, 1957), p. 5.

[2] Kenneth Cragg, *Christianity in World Perspective*, 2nd impression (London, 1969), p. 65.

in the first place, the shock of discovering other world religions on its doorstep. In the past, Christianity was able to determine the time, place, and conditions of an encounter with a non-Christian faith, and that encounter occurred on foreign soil. Now foreign cultures and religions, even so emphatically indigenous a system as Hinduism, are discovering their own potential of universal relevance and are in the process of developing it irrespective of Christian resentments. Yoga institutions, Buddhist circles, Ahmadiyya mosques are drawing followers from all walks of life in Western society. Eastern spirituality is advertised as vastly superior to anything the West may have to offer. Even so-called primitive religion is making its presence sharply felt. In Brazil, seemingly a Christian country, at least one-fifth of the population are said to adhere to new syncretistic cults in which African rites are gaining a new lease on life. All this severely jolts a Christian complacency that had been nourished on the conviction that foreign religions are moribund, and that Christianity would eventually possess all nations in their masses. Statistics have their limitations, but they do prove irrefutably that in numbers Christianity is steadily losing ground. As a result, there is a new appreciation of the view enunciated long ago by the History of Religion school of theology: Christianity has no claim to supernatural sanction and structural uniqueness beyond that of any other historical religion. If it is said to possess an absoluteness, it can only be a "relative absoluteness" (Ernst Troeltsch) — relative, that is, to the possible emergence of a superior religion in the future.

However, there is another side to the coin. If Christianity has been shocked by the fresh challenge of other world religions, non-Christian religions have been no less shocked by discovering Christianity in a new and more authentic sense. So long as the Christian gospel appeared on the Asian or African scene as just another corollary to Western imperialism and colonialism, it could be disregarded as the tribal cult of the white man. Either one might expect it to disappear together with colonial rule, or one might try to use its services for a better material life so long as one's own cultural and religious resources were not sufficiently developed. Chagrined missionaries would complain: "We thought that we were offering them Christ, and they

thought that we were offering them a school."[3] The very indi-
rectness of the impact of Christian faith on people and cultures
tended to immunize people and cultures against the faith rather
than make them more prone to conversion.

Yet Christianity did have an effect below the surface. And
when the colonial powers disappeared — not so Christianity and
its indigenous churches. Material development was supplied
much more effectively by agencies other than Christian missions. And in many areas the Christians were apparently prevented from making large-scale progress. But the fact that
Christ was still being offered by them could not but result in a
kind of spiritual unrest which the established leadership and
institutions of non-Christian faiths were often ill-equipped to
meet. The meaning of history, the importance of the individual,
his responsibility to act in the world — such were the questions
the Christian message had planted in many souls, and no non-
Christian religion could afford to neglect them.

There is another change deeply affecting both Christianity
and other religions, a shock which, though chronologically and
materially more closely related to the former than to the latter,
drives both of them to a new assessment of their positions in
human history. Whatever one may think of that "great new
common denominator of secularized circumstance in this time,"[4]
there is every reason to believe that its frontal assault against
all religion cannot be evaded. On the other hand there is as
much reason to believe that the unqualified joy with which the
discovery of the secular has been hailed in many Christian circles has passed its peak. Moreover, one suspects that at the very
heart of secularization a "re-religionization" (Georges Balan-
dier) may occur which renders the equation of modernity and
a-religiousness naive and futile. Be that as it may, the shock
must not be underrated. It should at least serve to show that
the encounter of Christianity and non-Christian religions has
become more urgent than ever before, and that it will tax the
awareness, imagination, and flexibility of all participants to a
degree unprecedented. Even secular futurology is today prepared to admit that "one cannot investigate the future of man-

---

[3] Bishop Whittaker of the Church of South India, quoted by Michael
Hollis, *Paternalism and the Church* (London, 1962), p. 3.
[4] Cragg, p. 169.

kind without investigating the future of religions."[5] The Christian world mission should share this concern, if only because its own future may be at stake.

II

Christianity enters the encounter with a handicap. Much as its spokesmen may be ready to abandon anachronistic structures of church organization and ways of witness, there is a hard core of nonnegotiable convictions which must not be surrendered. It is true that this has far too often been expressed in a dogmatic assertiveness and legalism, or even in a spirit of arrogant possessiveness, which renders Christ's invitation unworthy of belief. Clearly there is no single, timeless pattern of confessing loyalty to Christ irrespective of contextual factors. Nevertheless, when all is said and done, Christian witness cannot remain trustworthy unless certain elementary marks of identity are recognizable.

First, the Christian faith remains under a missionary mandate. This may mean something very different from what "missions" have stood for so far. It may, for example, include relinquishing the intention of adding to church membership. It may also mean being ready to expose oneself and one's cause to thorough scrutiny by the partner in dialogue, instead of making demands on him. It cannot, however, include concealing and suppressing the name of him who renders such a *diakonia* possible, who wants to be present in every Christian presence in order to make it transparent for his own saving purposes.

In fact, this is the second factor indispensable for the Christian partner in dialogue: Dialogue should be more than an exchange of information or opinions; its concern — though not necessarily explicit — should be the salvation and reconciliation wrought by God in Christ for all mankind.

This dialogue participates, thirdly, in the universality of reconciliation. It admits of no exclusive claims, no monopolies. In the words of David Chellappa, an Indian bishop, it invites "not to an exclusive museum of saints but to a universal asylum of sinners justified."

Therefore the Christian in dialogue is, finally, not called upon to sit in judgment over his partner. "The true evangelistic movement is not that I take Jesus Christ into somebody else's life,

---

[5] Georg Picht, *Mut zur Utopie* (München, 1969), p. 132.

but that Jesus Christ takes me into somebody else's life."[6] It is Christ who summons both the "giver" and the "receiver." In propaganda, in proselytism, it is a matter of justifying one religion over the other and drawing as many adherents of the other side as possible into one's own camp. In Christian dialogue it is primarily a matter of sharing God's justification of man with others. Christianity as a religion is at best instrumental, an "earthen vessel to show that the transcendent power belongs to God and not to us" (II Cor. 4:7).

III

In the light of what has been said so far, it should be possible to evaluate some current attempts to define the way in which Christians should encounter non-Christian religions. Four models deserve special attention.

1. The model of *addition*. Historically, any attempts to combine elements of non-Christian religions with Christianity have failed, partly because of the inherent incompatibility of the components and partly because of the underlying uncertainty which motivated the endeavor. While deliberate attempts of this kind are unlikely to be repeated, there are even today examples of a spontaneous growing together of new religious bodies out of elements of existing ones, including Christianity. In fact, such syncretistic processes can be expected to happen wherever living religions encounter each other. Perhaps they should even be considered evidence of the dynamism of religious history. However, such processes will inevitably generate new religions rather than partnerships in dialogue. Christianity, as the short history of Caodaism in Vietnam shows, is bound to lose its identity in the process.

2. The model of *reduction*. While in syncretistic processes the rule is "something of everything," the underlying principle of reduction is "all is one." Once a common denominator is found, the differences among religions become irrelevant. This seems to be the secret to the success of the proposals made by leading Hindu philosophers of religion like Dr. S. Radhakrishnan. If the essentials of all great religions can be reduced to mysticism, for example, nothing should stand in the way of a *unio mystica* of

---

[6] "The Evangelistic Situation," *Union Seminary Quarterly Review*, XV, 2 (January 1960), 114.

those religions. But attractive as this proposition is, it does not square with the phenomenology of religion. For while every living religion does possess traits analogous with traits in other religions, each religion nevertheless remains an entity in its own right despite such analogies. The trend of religious history is toward differentiation rather than uniformity.

3. The model of *evolution*. This idea was particularly popular among nineteenth-century theologians and philosophers of religion because it seemed to permit a comprehensive synopsis of religious history without abandoning the prerogative of Christianity, which conveniently figured as the highest stage in the religious development of mankind. While the results of modern history and phenomenology of religions have gone a long way in discrediting such a concept, it is being revived today by a strong movement in Roman Catholic theology, originating chiefly in the thought of Karl Rahner. All religions are taken to be provided by God as legitimate ways of salvation for those who follow them *bona fide*. Such people may even be regarded as "anonymous Christians." Whenever and wherever Christianity appears on the scene, it finds a ground well prepared for its ministry. Its task is not to eliminate but to awaken and fulfill what is already there in the depth of men's hearts. In that sense only is Christianity the absolute religion, and the church the place where full salvation is to be found (though not the exclusive community of the saved).

While this view has rightly been welcomed for its effectiveness in banishing arrogance and hardness of heart, it leaves at least one essential question unanswered: Why should adherents of other religions turn to the Christian gospel at all? If their religious acts, imperfect as they may be, are acceptable as worship of the living God leading to salvation, why make any additional demands upon them? Moreover, this scheme, too, is hardly compatible with a scientific view of religions and their distinctive characters. For non-Christian religions may not at all agree with the position assigned to them in a Christian pattern of the progressive evolution of salvation. They may well decline being fulfilled and perfected by the Christian gospel. Or, in other words, why should not the Hindu, instead of accepting his new status as an "anonymous Christian," demand that the Christian should become an anonymous Hindu?

4. The model of *absolutism.* Paradoxically, religions tend toward antagonism rather than coexistence, toward making rigorous claims of superiority rather than toward practicing tolerance and compromise. Christianity has been no exception. The history of Christian missions is replete with instances of such exclusiveness and intolerance. But no matter what happens among non-Christian religions — Hinduism, for example, while preaching universal brotherhood and tolerance to the rest of the world, is often unable or unwilling to grant a minimum toleration to Islam in its own neighborhood — Christianity is clearly obligated to extend an invitation rather than to announce condemnation and destruction, to hold out a hope rather than to deliver a demand for unconditional surrender. It must do so not only for expediency, although it cannot and must not ignore the shape of a coming world civilization, but primarily because Christians are to be ambassadors of the love and truth of Jesus Christ. Their double task is "openness to all in compassionate realism and openness to Christ as the one necessary loyalty."[7]

Thus neither an easy compromise nor the discovery of "anonymous Christians" nor an absolutizing of the Christian's own religious heritage can relieve him of the obligation both to take seriously the distinctiveness of other faiths and to loyally and expectantly mediate the Christian faith in the context of companionship and participation.

IV

Christian dialogue with non-Christian religions should be founded on both a deep sense of solidarity with non-Christians and a firm commitment to witness. These twin factors may often seem to lead in opposite directions, rather than offer an unequivocal directive. But in terms of Christian *diakonia,* there is the promise of overcoming such a dilemma by living with it in expectant obedience. Here, too, Dr. J. H. Oldham's famous ecumenical dictum merits fresh exploration: "We must dare in order to know."

Solidarity would, first, extend to all those problems concerning the task and shape of truly human existence in a rapidly changing world. The remarks made by M. M. Thomas during

---

[7] Cragg, p. 85.

the 1963 World Missionary Conference at Mexico City are as pertinent today as they were then:

> There is a growing sense of common humanity or human solidarity in the world which finds its expression in mutual concern, a sense of participation in the struggles of others for their fundamental rights, and a common endeavour in building structures of a world community and searching for an ethos to make them stable. This "secular ecumenical movement" may be only beginning, but it is already a genuine movement of human solidarity which we must recognize as a new factor of no small significance in the world today.[8]

Religions, Christianity included, have certainly been slow in recognizing a responsibility in this field. If they have recognized it, they have normally applied it to their own constituency only. But there are notable exceptions. In India, the Christian minority has set an example by foregoing their claim to separate parliamentary representation, thus opening the way for noncommunal participation in nation-building. No modern secular state can exist without that kind of cooperation from all its citizens regardless of their religious loyalties. The breakup of the traditional integration of religion with political, economic, and social institutions for the sake of the greater good of all must not be left to the forces of secularism. It should become the concern of the religions themselves, even if sacrifices are involved. The great universal issues of economic development and social justice offer even more pertinent examples. Scientists are agreed that world hunger cannot be avoided except by a drastic increase in production and by birth control. It is the latter which in certain parts of the world may prove to be a major test of the willingness of religions to abandon what may have been part of their social philosophy, for the benefit of the whole family of mankind. In any case, it is likely that in the future religions will be measured not only by the depth of their spirituality but by their loyalty to the dynamism of social change, justice, and peace.

Religions might be tempted to leave all this to the irresistible power of secularization while contenting themselves with safeguarding restricted spiritual areas as long as they can. This,

---

[8] *Witness in Six Continents* (London, 1964), p. 15.

however, would be a fatal misreading of what the situation really calls for. While secularism has brought to secular areas of life a certain integrity deserving the support of religions, it has also revealed its inability to provide the spiritual foundation without which the struggle for a new social humanism would be meaningless. This world of ours is largely man-made, and it is man who will produce the world of tomorrow. This cannot be done without responsible planning lest the world of the future end in self-destruction. But there can be no responsible planning without responsible people and institutions drawing their strength from resources which neither they themselves nor the world can supply. "The kind of insight which reason cannot gain on its own strength but by which reason is itself conditioned is what, in the language of faith, is called revelation."[9] So there is the exciting prospect of a world in which non-Christian religions, the Christian faith, and secular faith are not only called upon to coexist but also to cooperate in building a common society and culture.

Does this mean, as, for example, M. M. Thomas seems to suggest,[10] that the traditional walls between the religions have at last been broken down? His argument is striking: In the past the great non-Christian religions rejected Christian answers because they did not ask the questions for which Christianity had the answers. Today, under the pressures of secularism, the religions have begun to ask the questions about human existence and salvation to which the gospel gives the answer. But one wonders whether the non-Christian religions would be prepared to share this view, or whether they would not perhaps insist that ultimately their answers are different from those of the gospel, in spite of all necessary and legitimate coexistence and cooperation with Christianity. It is indeed tempting to imagine that the new prospects of interreligious solidarity will eventually reduce the differences between religions to a trifle. Yet an objective study of religions would show that this is most probably not the case. Even today it is not the minor things in which religions differ but the great issues concerning existence, the meaning of life and death, and man's eternal destiny. Whether we like it or not, it does make a difference that the

[9] Picht, p. 140.
[10] *Ibid.*, p. 19.

Buddhist strives for Nirvana, the Vedantin aspires to identity with Absolute Being, the Muslim seeks resignation to the overpowering will of Allah, and the Christian relies on justification by faith in Christ. Both in the interest of the Christian faith and of the truth as the various religions see it, it is imperative to leave room for an open and uncompromising dialogue on ultimate concerns. Dialogue it must be because the obligation to "openness in compassionate realism" is inescapable. Ultimate concerns must be respected lest the dialogue trail off into trivialities. Perhaps "exchange" is a better, less technical term, allowing for both more passion and more commitment.[11] At any rate, for the Christian this is the occasion where witness is to come into its own.

Let it be said immediately that even here solidarity is by no means suspended. In the process of dialogue or exchange this means, in particular, that controversy as an end in itself must be avoided just as studiously as debates about peripheral things. Christian apologists have sometimes been at pains to encounter the other religion at its worst, so that by contrast their own position is certain to emerge favorably. It should be obvious that this serves no purpose at a time when through the pressures of secularism all religions are facing an unprecedented crisis of judgment. The Christian task in dialogue should rather begin with a deep understanding of God's judgment on any religion and religious observance, including the Christian religion. There are elements of scepticism and uncertainty in every religion. But Christianity is probably better equipped than any other religion to press beyond this, beyond conventional lamentations about the cracks and flaws in human spirituality, to a deeper awareness of man's inability to justify himself before God even by means of his most subtle and profound religious efforts.

It is at this point that the message of redemption assumes its full meaning — redemption not as an achievement of man and his religious or nonreligious aspirations but as the free gift of God in Christ. Again the Christian task in dialogue would be sorely misunderstood if solidarity were replaced by a magisterial dispensation of graces that Christians, their community, and their religion claimed to hold in firm possession. As long as the Christian partner in dialogue aims at defending the absolute-

---

11 See John V. Taylor, *CMS Newsletter,* No. 328, June 1969.

ness of his religious beliefs, the result will be a closing of ranks and minds which paralyzes the exchange before it has really begun. The lesson of a recent experiment in Hindu-Christian dialogue in India should be heeded: "Our faith challenges us to risk our faith. As long as we are not ready to stake our own nearness to Christ for our brethren we do not know the meaning of faith."[12] On the other hand, if and when dialogue reaches the level at which both partners are exposed not only to judgment but to the light of love and redemption, to an absolute which claims both of them, both may be able to experience a transforming power which transcends the religious possibilities of either.

Dialogue, as Paul Tillich has said, implies "a mutual judging which opens the way for a fair valuation of the encountered religions and quasi-religions."[13] But is that the only consequence? Tillich and many others would maintain that, whatever else may happen, there is no justification for the Christian to hope that his partner may be converted. Now if conversion were to mean a change from one kind of religious self-assertion to another, it would indeed be undesirable. But do we dare to restrict the sovereign freedom of God to bring people to the obedience of faith? Can we exclude from any serious dialogue the hope that it may be used as an instrument not only of mutual criticism and enlightenment but also of a transformation that affects religious loyalty in its totality? "The outcome of the dialogue is the work of the Spirit," declared the ecumenical "Consultation on Dialogue with Men of Other Faiths" at Kandy, 1967.[14] The very openness without which there can be no dialogue should include openness for conversion as a possible outcome of dialogue. It is unfortunate that the question of conversion as "an inner spiritual and moral rebirth, a radical turning to God" — to use again the phraseology of the Kandy declaration — is too often confused, within the church and outside of it, with the problem of the chances of Christianity as a religion among others. An exclusively "expansionist" view of the future

---

[12] Klaus Klostermaier, *Christ und Hindu in Vrindaban* (Köln, 1968), p. 140.

[13] *Christianity and the Encounter of the World Religions* (New York, 1963), p. 94.

[14] *International Review of Mission*, LVI, 223 (July 1967), 340, 343.

of the Christian mission should indeed be exposed by Tillich's remark that, just as a *mixture* of religions would destroy in each of them the concreteness which gives it its dynamic power, "the victory of *one* religion would impose a particular religious answer on all other particular answers."[15] It is in this area more than in any other that conventional views of the Christian mission need revision. Are we prepared to understand that conversion to Christianity is not necessarily conversion to Christ? Are we ready to believe that the mission and dialogue of Christ's church may entail serving non-Christian religions in love? We are perhaps only beginning to recognize questions such as these, without knowing the answers. Meanwhile we may find guidance and wisdom for our dialogue in what one of the greatest of missionaries, Roland Allen, wrote more than half a century ago:

> Christ is hidden there in heathen lands and we go to seek Him. In revealing Him to others we reveal Him to ourselves. We give not as a wealthy man may give to the poor of his abundance ... but as he gives who scatters his seed upon a rich field, looking for a harvest in which both he and those for whom he labours will find their life.[16]

---

[15] *Ibid.*, p. 96.
[16] Roland Allen, *Missionary Principles* (Grand Rapids, 1964), p. 98.

KOSUKE KOYAMA is a minister of The United Church of Christ in Japan and also the Church of Christ in Thailand. He graduated from Tokyo Union Theological Seminary, received his B.D. degree from Drew Theological Seminary, and his Th.M. and Th.D. degrees from Princeton Theological Seminary. He taught at Thailand Theological Seminary from 1961 to 1968. Presently he is a member of the World Council of Churches Faith and Order Commission and he serves as Executive Director of the Association of Theological Schools in South East Asia, editor of the *South East Asia Journal of Theology,* and Dean of the South East Asia Graduate School of Theology. He is the author of *In the Land of Mendicant Monks and Water-buffaloes,* in Japanese, as well as a *Commentary on the Lord's Prayer, The Good News of God and the Conduct of Christians, What the Bible Says about Work, What Did the Apostles Preach?* and a *Companion to Karl Barth's Dogmatics in Outline,* all in the Thai language as theological handbooks in the Theological Education Textbook Programme. He has also contributed scholarly articles to the *South East Asia Journal of Theology, The Indian Journal of Theology, Practical Anthropology,* and the *International Review of Mission.*

3

Kosuke Koyama: "Gun" and "Ointment" in Asia

... and the house was filled with the fragrance of the ointment.
(John 12:3)

IN THIS PAPER I SHOULD LIKE TO EXAMINE THE HISTORY OF THE Christian mission in Asia, and in doing so invite the reader to see its implications for the future of missions there. The paper will have three sections. First I must try to place Asia in historical perspective, keeping missiological concerns in mind. There are various ways to formulate this perspective and consequently various perspectives. I propose to locate Asia in the perspective of the West's "gun" and "ointment," its wounding and healing — for the West has meant both for the East.[1] In the second section I will examine the sense of participation in world history that Asians have developed in response to the

---

[1] How to determine the historical and theological whereabouts of Asia involves great debates. How is Asia's own history to be assessed vis-à-vis the message of Israel and the church? Was the history of Asia experienced prior to the coming of the *kerygma* of Christ not "fully" history? Only marginal to the "real" history? What is the theological meaning of the words "prior to"? What is the theological understanding of the enduring value of the great Asian civilizations? General Simatupang of Indonesia finds Lesslie Newbigin's assessment of Asians as " 'people who have no history' before the experience of the modern Western invasion" difficult to accept (Alan C. Thompson, "Faith and Politics: The Indonesian Contribution," *The South East Asia Journal of Theology* [Spring 1970]. See also Lesslie Newbigin, "The Gathering Up of History into Christ," *The Missionary Church in East and West,* ed. C. C. West and D. M. Paton [London, 1959]).

impact of the West. And in the final section I will suggest how the Christian mission should respond to the Asia of today.

I. THE "GUN AND OINTMENT" PERSPECTIVE

It was in 1511. The Portuguese fleet, incited by greed after their monopoly of the Asiatic trade and by hatred for the infidel Muslim, approached the fortress of Malacca. The captain of the fleet, Alfonso de Albuquerque, spoke to his men to inspire them on the eve of their assault on the city. The speech contains a highly interesting theological interpretation of the event.

> It is, too, well worthy of belief that as the King of Malacca, who has already once been discomfited and had proof of our strength, with no hope of obtaining any succour from any other quarter — sixteen days having already elapsed since this took place — makes no endeavour to negotiate with us for the security of his estate. Our Lord is blinding his judgment and hardening his heart, and desires the completion of this affair of Malacca.[2]

But contrary to Albuquerque's imperialistic theologizing, I am afraid that God hardened *his* heart and blinded the judgment of King D. Manuel. The heart of the Portuguese captain was hardened, first, by his drive after wealth and his antipathy for the Muslims, and perhaps second, by the very direct application of a biblical doctrine — a doctrine which happens to be a most controversial and abstruse one, not to be used without soul-searching — to his historical situation, for his own advantage. The guns he carried on his fleet symbolized the first hardening, the cross he hoisted high on his fleet symbolized the second. Albuquerque was convinced that God Almighty was on his side. He was hardened to a degree unknown to the Asians, who lacked the "theological maturity" to utilize biblical doctrine to their advantage![3]

---

[2] H. J. Benda, J. A. Larkin, *The World of Southeast Asia* (New York, 1967), p. 78.

[3] An historical and theological investigation of the origin and development of the European background of the "aggressive theology" up to the appearance of Albuquerque in the East would be a worthwhile study. The church's negative attitude toward Jews and Moslems, and her ability to suppress other religious persuasions, certainly must have related to the eventual appearance of Albuquerque. But we cannot take up this discussion here.

Malacca 1511 stands as an incident full of symbolic historical value. In the person of Albuquerque one can discern the whole structure and character of the relationship between Asia and the West. In her dealing with Asia, the West has often been hardened by commercial avariciousness and by theological self-righteousness. These two "hardening" elements constitute the main ingredients of the gunpowder of the West against Asia. Professor K. M. Panikkar's *Asia and Western Dominance* is an extensive historical investigation of the acts of the West's "gun" since May 27th, 1498, the day the *San Gabriel* arrived at Calicut. Whether we begin in 1498, or in 1511, or in 1564 (the time of the first Spanish settlement in Cebu by Miguel Lopez de Legaspi), or in 1602 (the time of the formation of the Dutch United East India Company, to which "was granted the monopoly of trade in the regions between the Cape of Good Hope and the Magellan Straits for an initial period of twenty-one years, together with power to make treaties, build forts, maintain armed forces and install officers of justice"), we can discern the same psychological structure in the West's aggression on Southeast Asia.[4] The history of "the new power" (K. M. Panikkar) since the sixteenth century involves extremely complicated historical processes and accidents which differ significantly from one locality to another. An economic, anthropological, and cultural assessment of Asia's experience with Western expansion, conquest, and empire-building from 1498 to 1914 poses a formidable scientific assignment. The point I wish to make here is that the twenty cannon mounted on the deck of the *San Gabriel*, flagship of the Vasco da Gama expedition, meant far more than some twenty mechanical arrangements in which gunpowder could be ignited. They symbolized the coming of a time of radical crisis and upheaval for Asian life, the shaking up of her economic, political, and cultural life. This was a process of "wounding," particularly as it came at the hands of the countless "hardened and blinded" Albuquerques!

But concomitant with the "gun" there came also "ointment." "From the same mouth come blessing and cursing," as the Epistle of James says (3:10). And in the West's relationship with Asia, history has produced both "blessing and cursing" in

---

[4] Daniel G. E. Hall, *A History of South-East Asia* (New York, 1968), p. 271.

a remarkable fashion. Sixteenth-century Europe has the distinction of being the century in which both "wounding" and "healing" began to reach the East. It was a stormy century for the European nations in their political, religious, and scientific life, accelerating the momentous transition from the medieval to the modern periods which took place between the twelfth and eighteenth centuries.

What "healing" did the West bring into Asia, perhaps as an "unintended gift" of the age of Albuquerque?[5] *Modernization.* The modernization of Asia has been a long process, reaching its greatest acceleration since the Second World War. Modernization does not mean simply the spread of modern technological information and practice. It is a new orientation in the life of mankind that has been effecting radical transformations in all areas of human life. It expresses its effects in political systems, international life, community life, education, health service, employment, labor conditions, public works, and business enterprises. It can change the very values of a culture.[6] Professor C. E. Black defines modernization as "the process by which historically evolved institutions are adapted to the rapidly changing functions that reflect the unprecedented increase in man's knowledge, permitting control over his environment, that accompanied the scientific revolution."[7]

As a result of modernization, Asians have come to a new conviction about history. First, they are becoming increasingly convinced that they can be the main force in the universal history of mankind today and tomorrow. Through their active participation in history, they can *change* history. Second, they are becoming convinced that history has a definite goal. In modernization they have found a practical goal toward which to purposefully move. An "Asia Drama" has begun, as Gunnar Myrdal has called it. Outwardly, the "modernization ointment" has increased physical comfort in everyday life. Inwardly, it has generated a sense of active participation in history.

---

[5] "It is a rather striking peculiarity of Western colonialism that, although there are many flagrant episodes of 'naked imperialism', it has had in various directions a stimulating influence on the East, to a quite amazing degree" (Hendrik Kraemer, *World Cultures and World Religions* [Philadelphia, 1961], p. 67).

[6] Gunnar Myrdal, *Asian Drama*, I (New York, 1968), 73.

[7] *The Dynamics of Modernization* (New York, 1966), p. 7.

Modernization, however, is not all ointment. This becomes clear when one studies one of the main arteries through which the blood of modernization circulates in the world today — technological advancement. Technology, from the printing machine of Gutenberg in 1448 to the American moon walk in 1969, has to a significant extent emancipated mankind from toil and suffering. It has succeeded in putting an astonishing amount of educational material into the hands of millions. It has achieved miracles in hospitals. Technological advancement stands in a positive relationship with the "life abundant" for which Christ came (John 10:10; Matt. 11:4-6). But unhappily it is also technology that transformed the twenty guns mounted on the deck of the *San Gabriel* to the nuclear missiles delivered by underwater submarines. The cannons of the *San Gabriel* have by the apocalyptic touch of technology become cosmic guns. Technological efficiency, no matter how fantastic, with all its computers, heart transplants, nuclear energy, cannot by itself solve the problem of history. Isn't there a demonic alliance between the technocratic psychology and the modern age? "The modern age, more than any other, has been an age of assassinations, of civil, religious, and international wars, of mass slaughter in many forms, and of concentration camps,"[8] notes Professor Black. Between 1820 and 1949 the world lost 46.8 million lives in wars.[9] This is "the agony of modernization."[10] Modernization itself, then, must be realistically understood as both "gun and ointment." "Colonial gun and modernization ointment" and "modernization ointment and modernization gun" are continuous, coexisting, and mixed.

II. HISTORY-PARTICIPATION AND THE CHRISTIAN MISSION

Prior to the invasion of the West's "gun and ointment," Asia lived isolated in the great histories of her own nations, empires, and civilizations. Perhaps due to the abruptness and speed of the Western invasion of the East, the modern world has not had the time and concentration to grasp the vast and profound achievement of Asian civilizations. The sons of Asia, Gotama

---

[8] *Ibid.*, p. 27.
[9] *Ibid.*, p. 33.
[10] *Ibid.*, p. 26.

Siddhattha, the writers of the Upanishads, Confucius, and Lao-tse participated in the "axial" period of mankind with Elijah, Isaiah, Jeremiah, Deutero-Isaiah, Zarathustra, Homer, Parmenides, and Plato. Hazarding a limited characterization of Asia's response to history, I would say that it has been a response of *patience*, in contrast with the West's *impatience*. The strongly linear view of history based on the biblical tradition that God is the Governor of history is not indigenous to the life and thought of the peoples of South and East Asia. The linear sense, when appropriated by the man of *hybris*, can produce a dangerous *impatience* with history.

The biblical God is the God who "experiences" history.[11] He has his purpose for the history of man. He does "strange things" in history (Isa. 28:21). He may harden the mind of man according to his purpose. Albuquerque became *theologically impatient* with the city of Malacca, since he was convinced that God, in his holy zeal, was on his side. The Albuquerquean impatience and aggressiveness are thus of a special kind, since they have a theological foundation.[12] Yet for the mortal Albuquerque to say that God was on his side and blinding the judgment of his enemy was a distorted and egoistic expression of the biblical view of history. The relationship between the mystery of hardening one's heart and the mystery of the linear view of history is an extremely dangerous area for speculative man to walk in.

In July of 1937 this Albuquerquean theistic impatience was given powerful expression in the East by atheist Mao Tse-tung.

> In the present epoch of the development of society, the responsibility of correctly knowing and changing the world has been placed by history upon the shoulders of the proletariat and its party. This process, the practice of changing

---

[11] "What concerns the prophet is the human event as a divine experience. History to us is the record of human experience; to the prophet it is a record of God's experience" (Abraham J. Heschel, *The Prophets* [New York, 1962], p. 172).

[12] For example, in 1454 Henry the Navigator received a bull from Pope Nicholas V announcing the following: "... We, after careful deliberation, and having considered that we have by our apostolic letters conceded to King Alfonso, the right, total and absolute, to invade, conquer and subject all the countries which are under rule of the enemies of Christ, Saracen or Pagan ..." (quoted in K. M. Panikkar, *Asia and Western Dominance* [London, 1959], p. 27).

the world, which is determined in accordance with scientific knowledge, has already reached a historic moment in the world and in China, a great moment unprecedented in human history, that is, the moment for completely banishing darkness from the world and from China and for changing the world into a world of light such as never previously existed.[13]

Mao here speaks theological language. The *kairos* has come through his "proletariat ointment"! And Mao is summoning his audience to change not only Asia but the entire world! His interpretation of and participation in history is based on the impatient criticism made by Marx and Lenin of the economic substructure of the West's "gun and ointment." Mao's passion and conviction in history betray their "Christian origin." His proletariat ointment is a great historical agent bringing revolutionary change into Asian life today.

Mahatma Gandhi's life (1869-1948) was a continuous story of active participation in history. He organized campaigns of civil disobedience, he was imprisoned because of his conviction about the direction of history, he founded the *ashram*, he advocated *swaraj* (home rule), he improved the status of the untouchables. He understood, through his own life and the life of his people, the whole range of implications the West's "gun and ointment" had for India. But his response, unlike Mao's, was a response of patience. He presented to the millions of his fellow Indians the *"ahimsa* ointment" (non-killing, non-violence), the first principle in the *satyagraha* (holding to the truth) movement.[14] The *ahimsa* ointment practiced by the Hindu Indian has been repeatedly referred to by U Thant, Secretary-General of the United Nations and a Buddhist:

It was in an effort to assert the dignity and worth of the human person that Gandhiji started the first passive re-

---

[13] From Mao's philosophical essay "On Practice," in *Essential Works of Chinese Communism* (New York, 1969), p. 95.

[14] The *satyagraha* movement "is an attempt to carry this ancient Indo-Aryan idea into play against what would seem to the eye to be the vastly superior powers of the highly mechanized, industrially supported, military and political equipment of the Anglo-Saxons' victorious machine of universal empire" (Heinrich Zimmer, *Philosophies of India* [New York, 1951], p. 169).

sistance movement called Satyagraha in South Africa at the beginning of this century. As its connotation so clearly shows, Gandhiji believed that the weapon of truth, if firmly grasped and purposefully used, could lead to peaceful change without resort to violence. This was indeed one of the great ideas of our century. Gandhiji has rightly been regarded as the apostle of Ahimsa or non-violence, a concept enshrined in the teaching of practically all the great religions. It is really one of the basic tenets of my own religion, Buddhism. Intolerance, violence and the spirit of persecution are foreign to Buddhism. . . . A familiar phrase one often hears is that "the end justifies the means." Gandhiji categorically rejected this idea; he did not believe that a noble end could be achieved by ignoble means.[15]

The *ahimsa* ointment is rooted in man's conscience and echoes the message of the axial epoch; at the same time, it is most relevant to the violently torn world of today. Secretary-General U Thant endorsed the *ahimsa* ointment as enshrined in "all the great religions" and "in line with the principles and purposes of the charter of the United Nations."[16] Another contemporary champion of the *ahimsa* ointment was Martin Luther King, Jr. — who like Gandhi also ironically suffered a violent death.

I have chosen two Asian ointments, centered in the two great countries of ancient Eastern civilization, China and India, whose spiritual and cultural influence upon the whole of Asia has been immense and profound. I have not intended to be comprehensive. There may be several other important Asian ointments. But the proletariat ointment and the *ahimsa* ointment are certainly among the most crucial elements with which the Christian mission must deal in this part of the world.

These ointments are two outstanding examples of Asian participation in history. They are not simply ideas. They have influenced millions of people in a concrete way. They have intended to heal the wounds of man. As I have noted, both ointments have come out of frictions and irritations with the West. The Asians are deeply aware of Western expansionism

---

[15] "Non-Violence and World Peace," *Gandhi Centenary Celebrations: Singapore* (Singapore, 1969), p. 15.
[16] *Ibid.*

and modernization. They are also acutely aware of the "missionary ointment," which is trying to heal the wounds of history in the name of a man crucified two thousand years ago. But while the missionary ointment has influenced, to a great measure, their commitment toward establishing social justice in the community of man, the name of Jesus Christ is not central to them. In fact they are bitterly critical of both modernization and missionary ointment. They see, rightly or wrongly, that neither the missionary ointment nor the modernization ointment has really healed the wounds of history. Modernization is valuable, says the *ahimsa* ointment, only so long as it increases the *ahimsa* value. It is valuable, says the proletariat ointment, only so long as it contributes to the creation of the classless society. The same is true of the missionary ointment.

The proletariat ointment positively accepts the proposition "the end justifies the means" because it is intensely "impatient" with history. In fact, its rejection of religious value is rooted in precisely the same impatience. The religious interpretation of and participation in history is too lenient and patient. The Chinese proletariat eschatological movement wants to engage in a radical surgery of history. It wants to cut history open, put its hand inside, and extract the cancer of all evils from the body of history once for all! The *ahimsa* ointment, reflecting the ancient Indo-Aryan tradition, does not work according to the historical scientific dialecticism. It is not impatient with history. It wants to speak to the history of man through a simple *satyagraha*. It proposes to "hold all things" (Col. 1:17) by the invisible power of the eternal truth.

Against the background of the proletariat ointment ("impatient" in the tradition of Albuquerque) and the *ahimsa* ointment ("patient" in the tradition of the ancient Indo-Aryan spirituality), a critical event took place in 1964. At its Sinkiang test ground, "impatient" China successfully detonated a device containing thermonuclear material. Sinkiang 1964 stands out as the Chinese transition from the proletariat ointment to the naked force of the modernization gun which was, until then, the monopoly of the West. China's apocalyptic gun has begun to drown out her message of "completely banishing darkness from the world." Her cosmic gun has become a threat to mankind because of her ideologically impatient position that "the end justifies the means." India, land of the *ahimsa* ointment, has watched the coming of the modernization gun to her neighbor and has felt seriously threatened by it. She has even begun to explore the possibility of developing nuclear arms herself, despite the devastating cost this project would entail. This move is a tragic departure from the *ahimsa* ointment to the *himsa* gun. The demonic fumes of the modernization gun are now beginning to paralyze the nervous system of the two centers of Asian civilization. The modernization gun will quickly expend the resources for the projects of the modernization ointment. In the place of the Albuquerquean exploitation and disruption has come slavery to arms expenditure. The West's positive contribution of the modernization ointment is going on, but under the constant threat of the super-gun. How long can the modernization gun and modernization ointment stay together in this crowded history of mankind today?

III. THE HISTORY-PARTICIPATION OF THE ANOINTED ONE

From the sole of the foot even to the head, there is no
soundness in it, but bruises and sores and bleeding wounds;
they are not pressed out, or bound up, or softened with oil.
(Isa. 1:6)

In the house of Simon the leper at Bethany a nameless woman broke a jar of costly ointment and poured it over the head of Jesus. Her act was a symbol of the impending death of the Anointed One. Jesus responded: "And truly, I say to you, wherever the gospel is preached in the whole world, what she has done will be told in memory of her" (Mark 14:9). Wherever the gospel is preached — in China, Hong Kong, Vietnam, Cambodia, Laos, Thailand, Malaysia, Singapore, Indonesia, the Philippines, Burma — what she did will be told in memory of her, because she staged a symbolic act demonstrating the substance and manner of God's participation in history. The Crucified One (I Cor. 2:2) is the form of God's participation in history. The fragrance of God's history-creation, history-participation, history-government, and history-fulfillment in Christ must fill the whole *oikoumene*. The substance of the missionary ointment is the entire story of God's work in man's history, culminating in the death and resurrection of Jesus Christ. Not historical judgment, but only theological discernment will reveal the missionary ointment's unique historical reality before one's eyes (II Kings 6:17; Mark 8:24f.). The history of the missionary ointment takes place *incognito* and patiently in the same history which other ointments activate.

Isn't it the function of the missionary ointment to soften the other ointments with the oil of God's judgment and salvation and let them participate in the movement of history of the missionary ointment? If God's participation in history is portrayed in the form of the Crucified One, the *morphe* of absolute self-denial, in order to issue the mightiest invitation to all "on earth or in heaven" (Col. 1:20), if the Lamb of God (John 1:29; Rev. 5:12) is the Victorious Head of the *ekklesia* and *cosmos* (Col. 1:15-20), then should not the missionary ointment work toward the realization of *koinonia* among the ointments participating in history together?[17] Can we find any ointment at work in history which is totally healing and completely free from any possibility of wounding, be it modernization ointment, *ahimsa* ointment, or proletariat ointment? In fact, is even the missionary ointment free from impurity? Isn't it true that there have been unfortunate incidents indicating entanglements, willing or unwilling, between the missionary ointment and the conquest-expansion gun?[18]

---

[17] The following theological position betrays a gross oversimplification of the theological and historical issues involved and is strongly reminiscent of the Albuquerquean theology: "Millions of Asians need to be delivered from the bondage of Satan, and millions of the spiritually hungry need the Bread of Life. At the same time, great giants like communism, the resurgent religions, materialism, and the cult of science are lifting their unholy fists against the most high God in ugly mockery and cynicism" (*Christ Seeks Asia,* official reference volume, Asia-South Pacific Congress on Evangelism, p. 155). This cannot be the way Christ seeks Asia.

[18] In 1857 the execution of the Spanish Bishop of Tongking, Mgr. Diaz, by the Vietnamese ruler Tu-Duc (1848-83) gave France a long-awaited pretext for seizing territory in Annam. At Hue, de Montign presented three demands to Tu-Duc, one of which was "a guarantee of religious liberty for Christians." A war ensued. In June 1862 a treaty was signed at Saigon "by which Tu-Duc ceded to France three eastern provinces of Cochin China and agreed to pay a heavy indemnity in instalments over ten years. He promised the free exercise of the Catholic religion in his dominions and to open the ports of Tourane, Balat and Kuang-An to French trade" (Hall, *A History of South-East Asia,* p. 613). Speaking of "the fortunes of Chris-

Alternatively, don't other ointments have an admixture of the christological ointment, and unconsciously participate in the fragrance of Christ in history? Isn't it possible to say that the West's "gun and ointment" have stimulated the dormant Asian ointments and thus made them to be historical forces in the life of the Asian? If so, cannot the "gun and ointment" of the West since 1511 be viewed in the light of Ephesians 1:10?

> *He purposes in his sovereign will that all human history shall be consummated in Christ, that everything that exists in Heaven or earth shall find its perfection and fulfillment in him* .(Phillips translation.)

If so — if we look up to the one crucified under Pontius Pilate as the one who will fulfill history with all its "guns and ointments" — I wish to ask three related questions with regard to the future of the Christian mission in Asia: (A) What are the specific ways by which the Christian mission can increasingly agitate history in order to facilitate a healthy increase of modernization ointment? (B) Should the Christian mission attempt to Christianize the secular or non-Christian ointments? Rather, shouldn't it participate in these other ointments with the full and patient recognition that they may indeed have a role in God's plan for Asia? Are we sure that we are not Albuquerques who are eager (impatient!) to storm Hong Kong, Djakarta, Manila, Rangoon (and Buddhism, Hinduism, Islam and Animism) as though all these are infidel Malaccas (Hos. 9:7; Jer. 25:29)? Should we be less patient with history than God is? (C) Is it possible, particularly in these dangerous post-Sinkiang days, for the Christian mission to be "the salt of the earth" (Matt. 5:13) unless it lives and exists within the confusion of "guns and ointments"? Will the Christian mission find any other means to command the attention of the Asian millions than by frustrating all the "guns" and giving passionate encouragement to all the "ointments"? And how can the Christian mission do this unless it begins itself to live under "the sentence of death"?

---

tianity" in the Moluccas, Hall writes that they "depended almost entirely upon the military strength of the Portuguese" (p. 233). The missionary ointment dependent "upon the military strength of the Portuguese" was a disastrous corruption. The peoples of Ternate and Amboina (Ambon) rejected Christianity. With respect to China, I would like to call the reader's attention to pp. 136f. of Panikkar's *Asia and Western Dominance.*

For I think that God has exhibited us apostles as last of all, like men sentenced to death; because we have become a spectacle to the world, to angels and to men. We are fools for Christ's sake, but you are wise in Christ. We are weak, but you are strong. You are held in honor, but we in disrepute. . . . We have become, and are now, as the refuse of the world, the off-scouring of all things. (I Cor. 4:9-13.)

LOTHAR SCHREINER is lecturer in missiology and comparative religion at the Kirchliche Hochschule, Wuppertal and secretary for scholarships and missionaries' orientation with the Rheinische Mission, Wuppertal. From 1956 to 1965 he was a missionary in Indonesia, serving both as lecturer of New Testament and Greek and librarian at the Faculty of Theology of Nommensen University, Pematang Siantar, Sumatra. He studied at the universities of Tübingen and Münster and at Mansfield College, Oxford, where he took the Honour School of Theology. He received the M.A. from Oxford University, the Th.D. from Zürich University, and the *venia legendi* (habilitation) from Heidelberg University. He is co-editor and co-author of *J. G. Hamann's Hauptwerke erklärt*, 8 vols., *Das Bekenntnis der Batak-Kirche*, and *Adat und Evangelium*, habil. thesis, Heidelberg 1969. He has also contributed several articles to the *Concise Dictionary of the Christian World Mission*.

4

Lothar Schreiner: The Church in Northern Sumatra: A Look at Its Past and Future

(INCLUDING AN UNPUBLISHED REPORT OF N. M. WARD, 1846*)

I

IT IS ONE OF PROFESSOR BEAVER'S ACHIEVEMENTS TO HAVE MADE known to the English-speaking world the work of European missionary societies and the churches overseas that have grown out of their efforts. He decided to include in his series of missionary studies a volume on the Batak churches in Northern Sumatra,[1] about which very little has been written in English.[2] While the Rhenish Mission Society has made the most successful attempt to plant the Christian church among the Bataks, beginning in 1861, its missionaries were neither the first nor the only ones on the scene. Notable is the missionary exploration

[1] Paul Pedersen, *Batak Blood and Protestant Soul* (Grand Rapids, 1970). For a bibliography on Christianity in Sumatra see G. H. Anderson, ed., *Christianity in Southeast Asia* (New York, 1966), pp. 39ff.

[2] See Frank L. Cooley, *Indonesia: Church and Society* (New York, 1968), pp. 66-74; see also Th. Müller-Krüger, *Der Protestantismus in Indonesien* (Stuttgart, 1968).

* I acknowledge with thanks the kind permission of the Kon. Inst. voor Taal-, Land-, en Volkenkunde, Leiden, to publish this manuscript—No. H. 302.

of Henry Lyman and Samuel Munson, who were sent out by the American Board of Commissioners for Foreign Missions (A.B.C.F.M.) of Boston. These two men were killed on their first venture into central Batakland in 1834.[3]

Ten years before the Americans came the British Baptists.[4] Three missionaries settled on the west coast of Sumatra — Nathaniel Ward in Bencoolen, Richard Burton in Sibolga, and Charles Evans in Padang. Their arrival in 1829 is closely connected with British rule in the Malayan archipelago. Sir Stamford Raffles himself not only tolerated evangelism among the indigenous peoples but actually suggested to Burton[5] that he interest himself in the Bataks. Moreover, in 1824 he sent Burton and Ward on their way to explore the Silindung valley in central Batakland with the aim of starting a mission among the Bataks, who lived in the interior of Northern Sumatra around Lake Toba. This first missionary visit to the Bataks was financed by the British government. Naturally an official report was submitted, published in the *Transactions of the Royal Asiatic Society of Great Britain and Ireland*.[6] The report contains a comprehensive description of the Bataks as a people, including a travel journal and a paragraph about their religion. It does not, however, record anything about the encounter of the two men with the Bataks. For a report of that we must turn to the Serampore periodical *Friend of India*, which published a letter sent by Nathaniel Ward.[7] In it Ward vividly recounts how their party traversed the rugged mountains on their way from Sibolga to Silindung, and mentions the respectful reception they received from the population of Silindung.

More important for the beginnings of the Christian church, however, is an 1846 memorandum sent by Ward in response to the Netherlands Bible Society, which had asked about the state of Bible translation into the Batak language and had submitted six questions about the possibility of evangelizing the Bataks.

---

[3] See P. Pedersen, Part II.

[4] See Ernest A. Payne, *Southeast from Serampore* (London, 1945), pp. 38-56. Payne gives a comprehensive account of the Baptists' Mission to Sumatra.

[5] *Ibid.*, p. 45.

[6] I (London, 1827), 485-513.

[7] November 1824 edition; see E. Payne, pp. 46f., for a reprint of a part of Ward's letter.

This memorandum is recorded in slightly shortened form below.

Ward, who left the Baptist Missionary Society in 1828, had moved to Padang, the central place on the west coast, where he lived on his own resources. He had declined the proposals of his society to move to Ceylon or India and decided to stay on in Sumatra after the Sumatran Mission of the English Baptists had ended in 1825, when the island was returned to the Dutch.[8] Ward evangelized among the Malay population of Padang, translated portions of the Bible into Malayan,[9] and in 1844 seems to have finished a Malayan version of the New Testament.[10] His memorandum belongs to the latest evidence of his life.

N. M. WARD'S REPORT ON A VISIT TO THE CENTRAL BATAK-LAND IN 1824

Handschrift H 302 KITLV Leiden

"Padang 19th Sept. 1846

In acknowledging the receipt of your Missive of the 9th instant No. 1473 with two enclosures, I have the honor to submit the following remarks for the information of the Netherlands Bible Society.

In the year 1821-22 the late Richard Burton established himself at Sibolga as Missionary to the Battas at the expense of the English Baptist Missionary Society. He remained there with his family to the end of 1825 when he removed to Bengal and died in the upper provinces of that country in 1827. During his residence at Sibolga Mr. Burton was employed in acquiring the language, writing small tracts, compiling a dictionary, and trans-

---

[8] In a letter of February 1844, from Padang, Ward seems to apologize for having no hope for Baptist missionary work in Northern Sumatra. He writes: "I am sorry I can offer no prospect of an opening door for missions in Sumatra yet. The Dutch Government have extended their authority to almost every part of the island, and they are not friendly to any means of enlightening the people. Sumatra and Java, and every other part of the Netherlands Indies, except Borneo, are closed against all foreign missions by positive enactments, and for Borneo they are under restrictions which must render them nugatory. The only manner, in fact, in which the natives of these extensive countries can become acquainted with the word of truth is through the medium of the press" (*ibid.*, p. 53).

[9] "Versions of the Gospel of John, the Book of Genesis and a Harmony of Gospels have been completed" (F. A. Cox, *History of the Baptist Mission Society 1792-1842* [London, 1942], first published in 1842).

[10] Payne, p. 52.

lating portions of Scripture into the Batta language. When he quitted the island he took with him the whole of his manuscripts and although I made enquiry for them after his death I never learnt what became of them. I know however that he had made considerable progress in compiling a dictionary, and that he had translated the Gospel of John, for the printing of which measures had been taken in 1825 to procure a fount of Batta types.

In 1824, at the expense of the British Govt., I made a journey to the interior of the Batta country accompanied by Mr. Burton. Our object was to go as far as the district of Toba lying on the borders of a great lake in a Northwest direction from the Bay of Tappanoelie, and represented as the most populous part of the Batta lands and the residence of the principal Chief. After crossing a tripple chain of mountains covered with wood and interspersed here and there with Kampungs, we came to a clear open country populous and well cultivated. Here we took up our abode for some days, in the district of Silindong, at the house of a chief of one of the most central villages, and were extremely well received by the chiefs and people, to whom being the first white men ever seen in the country we became objects of great curiosity.

Silindong was a large cultivated valley covered with 20 or 30 populous villages, the houses large and well built and inhabitted by from 20 to 60 souls each. Some days after our arrival we had a great meeting with the chiefs at which perhaps 5 or 6000 persons were present. We were entertained with feasting and dancing after the customs of the country. We explained to them publicly the objects of our Mission, read to them tracts on the creation, on the ten commandments and on the way of Salvation, which we offered for their acceptance. They debated the subject in our presence with much appearance of reason and good sense and in conclusion offered their assistance and invited us to settle amongst them, saying they must become acquainted with our doctrines before they could accept them.

A few days after this meeting Mr. Burton was taken ill of dysentry and while he was confined to the house I made excursions with a Batta guide and a man or two of our own to various parts of the district. I was received every where with kindness and respect and should have been very happy to continue the journey to Toba had Mr. Burton recovered. He grew worse however and it became necessary to return with him to the coast. Shortly after our return but not before I had left Sibolga Mr. B. received a letter from the principal Chief Singa Manga Radja announcing a great failure of the Paddy crops in Toba in consequence of our not visiting him, and requesting us most earnestly to come without delay. I had however returned to Bencoolen and Mr. B. did not feel inclined to go alone. Of this journey a report was published in Bengal in the Friend of India but I have not seen a copy either in print or manuscript.

I have mentioned these circumstances to show the N. B. Society that an attempt to translate the Scriptures into the Batta language has already been made and that it would then even have been successful had it been properly persevered in. At that period however the Baptist Mission Society was disinclined to continue its labors on Sumatra, the Mahommedan Priests of Menangkabau were making rapid conquests among the Battas, the encouragement and support of the British Govt. on the transfer of its settlements here to his Netherlands Majesty necessarily ceased, and the Mission to the Battas consisting only of one member rendered perseverance hopeless. At present circumstances have changed. The object now to be effected by the N. B. Society under the Netherlands Flag, the conquest of Mohammedanism have ceased, one half the Batta lands are under the immediate rule of the Netherlands Govt. which can give free access and full protection to any one employed for the purpose, and as the acquisition of the language is an object of perhaps quite as much importance to Govt. as to the Society it is to be presumed such access and protection would not be withheld.

With reference to the printed questions of the Society I may offer the following remarks.

1. On the state of civilisation and the arts of reading and writing. The Battas it is well known are cannibals, yet not of the worst description. . . . Such horrid customs long made the Battas a terror to strangers and closed their country against all the curiosity of travellers; and we were not a little surprised on our visit to Silindong to find in their character a degree of mildness and timidity exceeding that of any other tribe on Sumatra.

Civilisation is a very relative term and according to its European acceptation is but little applicable to the Battas. Their wants are extremely few. Rice and salt are their principal food and a single piece of cloth for the generality of both man and woman serves to cover their nakedness. Hogs, fowls and cattle are luxuries generally reserved for the deities and the spirits of the dead. Money when I visited them was unknown, salt chiefly performing the office of exchange. Their houses were built of wood in a durable manner passing from one generation to another. The arts of weaving and dyeing coarse durable cloths were practised by the women. Tobacco was not in use but was known as an uncommon luxury, other herbs being employed instead in large brass smoking pipes. Opium was not known nor any strong drink in use for intoxication. Where the wants of a people are so very limitted it is certain there can be but little industry and where there is no industry it may be truly said — there can be no civilisation. According almost all labor is performed by the women who are in effect nothing better than slaves of the men.

The arts of reading and writing are known to the Battas but are practised only to a very limitted extent. The proportion who can read and write I should think, is not one in a thousand. Communications by letter from one person to another are occasionally made but very seldom and are then written or engraved on the joint of a Bamboo with the point of a knife or an iron style. They have however books written with ink on long strips of the inner bark of a tree folded in a zigzag form and covered with wood. These generally contain records of the superstitions of the country, prayers to their gods and devils, on occasion of war or sickness or of undertaking a journey or any thing of uncertain result, incantations, sorcery, witchcraft, and all the implements of knavery practised on the credulity of superstition. The history they retain of their great god Batara Goeru and a host of Debatas shews their religion to have descended from Hindoeism perhaps before the doctrines of the incarnations of the deities were introduced into Hindustan.

2. On the religious state of the Battas; whether the dissemination of the Bible would meet with opposition and whether any good result might be anticipated therefrom?

The Battas are perhaps the most superstitious people in the

world. They see a spirit in every tree, in every house, in every Kampung on the Rivers the Mountains the valleys the sea and the lakes are all full of spirits which they regard with awe, and dread as beings endued with power and often with a will to injure. Hence when at a distance from home they go armed with charms and incantations, they consult their spiritual guides and are ever on the look out with fears and trembling for marks of the anger of their spiritual enemies. The first enquiry of a large party we met on our way to Silindong was, with the most serious anxiety, whether we had seen any evil spirits on the road. Every place has its protecting deity who defends it from evil and avenges its injuries not only on transgressors themselves but on their relatives and descendants without limitation if they happen to come within the range of its power; and as no man knows where his forefathers may have committed offence he is equally ignorant where he may become the victim of spiritual vengeance. They have however no temples or stated religious worship. Idols I believe exist but are not common, temporary forms of their gods being made of plantain trees for particular purposes instead.

I am not of opinion that the distribution of the Bible would meet with any serious opposition from the Battas themselves. On the contrary I think there is far more success to be expected amongst them than among the Malays or any of the tribes converted to Mahommedanism. It is certain they have not that strong prejudice and antipathy to Christians and Christianity which is inseparable from Mahommedanism, and I think it is equally certain that as the power of Govt. extends over the country they will by degrees become converts to Mahommedanism unless previously brought over to Christianity. Being little under the influence of fixed principle, of belief upheld by a regular system of worship and the power of an interested priesthood, and feeling themselves inferior to both Europeans and the surrounding Mahommedans, the superstitions of the country will most likely fall to the first attempt made upon them.

The Society seems missinformed respecting the undersigned. I never was employed amongst the Battas. My station was Bencoolen where I had the management of the Printing-Press and the native schools. Since 1828 I have resigned all pecuniary support from the Society in England and been living on my own resources.

3. I am not aware that any material variety of dialect exist in the Batta language. It is said to be spoken by more than a million of souls and I believe the written and the spoken language is essentially the same all over the country.

4. I am not aware of any European or descendant of Europeans now living acquainted with the Batta language so far as to be able to render assistance in the translation of the Bible. I have already said that the manuscripts of Mr. Burton were taken by him to Bengal and that my enquiries for them after his death were unsuccessful. The Society might perhaps learn something of them by enquiring of the Secretary of the Baptist Mission Society London, or of J. C. Marshman Esq., Serampore, Bengal.

5. Nothing was ever printed in the Batta language nor were types or punches ever actually prepared and brought into use. This however would be a matter of no difficulty and no great expense. The system of writing is extremely simple. There are but about 20 consonants and half a dozen vowels. The letters of a word do not join or run into each other. The vowels are used in the same line as the consonants and not in separate lines above and below the consonants, as in the Malay and the Javanese, which makes printing in those languages extremely difficult and expensive. The system is originally of Sangskrit or Hindu origin brought into the Batta country perhaps before it had attained its present complicated improvements. Agreeably to that system each consonant contains the prevailing vowel sound of the language inherent in itself and constitutes a complete syllable without a vowel mark or letter. This greatly simplifies the mechanism and reduces the number of vowel letters required in composition. On the whole I should think thirty characters would be all the language requires, and as the letters are like our printed ones in not joining or running into each other the execution would be perfectly easy and the expense of printing not great.

6. In case of a person's being employed by the Society to gain the language and translate the Scriptures, the place of his residence should be left to his own judgement after making a survey of the country. It being supposed no one employed

would be deemed fit for the work unless he were willing to sac-
rifice many personal comforts and advantages, the choice of
place and local arrangements might be safely confided to himself. The importance of the object however, the length of time
required to execute it well, the uncertainty of European life in
this country, the slowness with which Europeans become im-
bued with oriental modes of thought and idioms of expression,
and consequently the great length of time requisite, under the
most favorable circumstances and with the best instruments,
to carry it into effect so as to make the work practically useful,
will suggest to the Society the question of risking success on
the life of a single individual. For myself I am of opinion such
work had better not be done at all than not be done well. On
the translation of the Bible in Malay neither time nor trouble
nor expense have been spared, and yet a version in that language intelligible to the natives may be still regarded as a
desideratum.

N. M. Ward

To
Major General Michiels,
Civil & Military Governor
of the West Coast of Sumatra"

II

Ward's memorandum and Ward as a resident of Padang link
the beginnings of Christian missions there with the later work
of the Rhenish Mission. As a missionary resident he welcomed
in 1856 the Dutch missionary G. van Asselt, who started evangelism in Sipirok, the southern part of Batakland, in January
1857,[11] and joined three Rhenish missionaries on Oct. 7, 1861,

---

[11] In his diary Van Asselt recalls his visit to Ward's home; and referring
to Ward's and Burton's encounter with the Bataks, he writes: "Since the
two were not entirely in command of the Batak language, they were misunderstood. When they spoke about the rebirth, for example, the Bataks
thought that as a people they had to grow small, poor, and low. A short
time later many of them were killed in the Padri war. The Bataks took this
disaster to be the fulfillment of the two missionaries' message, and when
Munson and Lyman came, the Bataks were afraid these white men would
bring with them another disaster. Hence they killed them, in 1834" (*Aus*

which has come to be regarded as the starting date of the Batak Mission and Church. It is very likely that Ward met L. I. Nommensen, the great pioneer-missionary among the Bataks, while Nommensen was at Padang in May-June of 1862.

In particular the memorandum proves that the Baptist mission to Sumatra was no isolated and ill-fated attempt, but the prologue to the great epic of evangelism in Northern Sumatra. This has to be substantiated with some details. Ward's memorandum was taken as a basis by the Netherlands Bible Society to send "an agent" to Batakland who would study the language in order to prepare a translation of the Bible. It was Herman Neubronner van der Tuuk (1824-1894), "the greatest expert for Indonesian languages" (H. Kern), who volunteered for this task.[12] He spent eight years (1849-1857) in Sumatra in order "to take a little torch to the Bataks," as he put it in his peculiar ironical manner. He produced a grammar and a dictionary of the Toba Batak language, as well as a translation of Genesis, Exodus, and the Gospel of John, to name only a few titles in his outstanding literary work.[13] After the uprising of the Dajaks in Kalimantan (Borneo) the Rhenish Mission Society decided to withdraw entirely from this island. In 1859 the head of the Rhenish Mission, Fr. Fabri, visited the Netherlands in order to discuss plans for future work with the Dutch missionary leaders. Waiting to see one of them, Fabri looked about some of the books on the table and his attention was drawn by a small book with a strange script; it turned out to be van der Tuuk's Batak translation of the creation story. Fabri went to see van der Tuuk to hear more about Batakland and returned to Wuppertal resolved to send missionaries to the Bataks. On October 26, 1860, the board

---

den Anfängen der Batak-Mission [Barmen, 1911], pp. 4f. English translation mine). This misunderstanding, if such it was, would explain the striking difference between the Bataks' attitude toward Burton and Ward in 1824 and toward Munson and Lyman ten years later.

[12] See H. N. v.d. Tuuk, *De pen in de gal gedoopt, brieven en documenten verzameld en toegelichtet door R. Nieuwenhuys* (Amsterdam, 1962); for a biography of this linguistic genius see the *Encyclopaedie van Nederlandsch Indie,* IV ('s-Gravenhage, 1921), 456ff. V.d. Tuuk was born in Malacca of a Dutch father and a Creole mother of Malacca.

[13] Together with H. Kern he laid the foundations for Malayan-Polynesian linguistics. For an evaluation of v.d. Tuuk's achievements as a linguistic scholar see P. Voorhoeve, *Critical Survey of Studies on the Languages of Sumatra* ('s-Gravenhage, 1955), pp. 99ff.

of the Rhenish Mission voted unanimously to begin in Northern Sumatra. In 1864 L. I. Nommensen settled in the Silindung valley, forty years after Burton and Ward had visited it.[14] In this way Ward's memorandum establishes the missing link in the history of Christianity in Northern Sumatra since 1824. While the British Baptists' Mission was not destined to continue after 1824, it paved the way for the successful undertaking of the Rhenish Mission after 1861.

The relevance of the memorandum may be outlined as follows. The members of the expedition were well prepared. They knew the languages. Burton had studied Batak, and Ward, Malay. Burton moreover had observed the customs and the way of life of the Batak for over three years. They intended to penetrate to the Singamangaradja, the High Chief of the Bataks, because they assumed rightly that he was the decisive head of the people, particularly in matters of religion.

On the one hand, the expedition was a success. The men were "extremely well received" and welcomed with the proper ceremonies, feasting, speeches, and dancing. They were given formal opportunity to explain their intentions and message. The whole procedure was performed in accordance with the local law, the Adat of the Bataks. Moreover they were invited to settle in Silindung and were offered assistance.[15] The Gospel-Speech included the creation story, the Ten Commandments, and, together with the "way of salvation" the facts of the life of Jesus.[16] The memorandum, twenty years after the event, points to another result of the expedition. It is important to note Ward's opinion that the distribution of Bibles would meet with far more success among the Bataks than it had among the Malays. He observes that he "found in the Batak character a degree of mildness and timidity exceeding that of any other tribe on Sumatra."

---

[14] As early as 1868, Fabri said that "the recent history of missions hardly knows a second example for such a peculiar and rapid advance of evangelism" (quoted from W. R. Schmidt, *Mission, Kirche und Reich Gottes bei Fr. Fabri* [Stuttgart, 1965], p. 175. English translation by the author).

[15] Contra P. Pedersen, p. 49. Pedersen's conclusion that in the end Ward's and Burton's approaches were rejected cannot be substantiated from the evidence.

[16] The details given by Warneck in *50 Jahre Batakmission* (1911), p. 14; by J. Sihombing in *100 Years Batak-Church* (in the Batak language) (1961), pp. 8ff.; and by P. Pedersen, are not sustained by the evidence of the expedition.

It is finally notable that Ward should suggest qualifications for the required Bible translator that fit so closely the extraordinary stature of van der Tuuk. In all, we find in the memorandum a well-balanced encouragement for the Netherlands Bible Society to take the translation of the Bible in hand soon.

On the other hand the expedition was a failure. Permission to settle definitely in the area rested largely with the High Chief Singamangaradja, who asked the missionaries to visit him. But Burton became ill, and they were prevented from doing so. And by not honoring the High Chief with a visit the men were thought to have provoked the wrath of the Batak gods. Therefore the High Chief asked them again to come to see him. But when his letter reached Burton in Sibolga, Ward had already left for Bencoolen. Burton did not want to make the visit by himself.

In the middle of 1825 Sibolga was severely threatened by the Padri sect, a conservative and aggressive Islam party from Minangkabau.[17] Burton asked Evans at Padang whether the Dutch intended to fight the Padris. When told that they did not, he decided to leave for Calcutta.[18] In the face of the Padri war (1825-1832), and in view of the return of Dutch rule in Sumatra, the Baptist Mission Society was disinclined to resume their work in Northern Sumatra. There was, however, a follow-up, late though it came — Ward's 1846 memorandum to the Dutch Bible Society.

To sum up, the English Baptists provided the material for the Dutch Reformed to produce the stepping stone for the German Mission Society to evangelize among the Bataks from 1861 to 1940. There is a joint action for mission in this record, and an ecumenical red thread in the texture of the beginnings of the Christian movement in Sumatra.

III

Christianity in Northern Sumatra has grown to include over a million members, and has become so thoroughly rooted among

---

[17] *Encyclopaedie v. Ned. Ind.*, III (1919), pp. 245ff.

[18] E. Payne quotes from a letter of Burton to Ward which makes it quite clear that Burton would have continued with his work at Sibolga under Dutch rule if there had been civil safety against the Padris (p. 49). Cf. Müller-Krüger, p. 252.

the Bataks as to make it the belief to have. On the whole, Christianity exhibits both the stronger and weaker aspects of a people's church. So powerful and persuasive is the customary law or Adat governing the life and destiny of man in this area,[19] that the Christian faith may seem to be simply its religious aspect. One is tempted to ask whether it isn't tribalism more than faith in the revealed God in Jesus Christ that accounts for the remarkable social coherence that strikes both the casual visitor and the resident fraternal worker from churches in other parts of the world. It may be said that the churches are on their way from people's churches to becoming gospel churches. Whatever dynamic progress there is points toward a fuller comprehension of what a church is and ought to stand for.[20]

The present outlook is very much determined by the missionary situation and opportunity. The Simalungun Batak Church (G.K.P.S.) has grown about 200 per cent in the last seventeen years, but still comprises only about a third of the Simalungun Batak people.[21] Great opportunities are opening, and the church is actively meeting them. There is the Karo Batak Church (G.B.K.P.), which since 1965 has grown almost too quickly for her to cope with. In the last four years so many heathen Karo Bataks have joined the church that every second member is a newcomer to the Christian faith.[22] In view of this rapid internal growth, the Karo Batak Church has concentrated her evangelistic efforts on her own people. For help she has turned to her sister churches in Indonesia. And thanks to a growing cooperative spirit, some ministers of other Indonesian churches were delegated to assist, instructing newcomers for baptism and membership.

A different missionary task is being assumed by the Toba

---

[19] See L. Schreiner, *Adat und Evangelium* (Gütersloh, 1971).

[20] This stage of progress is by no means a peculiar feature of "younger" churches in their second century. Präses Beckmann pointed out to the synodical meeting of the Evangelical Church in the Rhineland in January 1970 that "the break-up of the identity of church and society is a fact which is grievous for the church." He suggested that in this serious situation one ought to reflect on "What truly makes the church be the church" (*Westdeutsche Rundschau* [Wuppertal, 1970], pp. 2, 8).

[21] In 1968 she registered 85,000 members in 208 congregations served by 33 ministers.

[22] In 1965 she had 30,000 members; in 1969 she registered 77,000 members.

Batak Church (H.K.B.P.), the largest single church in Southeast Asia,[23] as she has begun a teaching and preaching ministry among the Zakai people and among Javanese on the east coast of Sumatra. She is also preparing an evangelistic ministry to the many Chinese of this area. In this missionary engagement she is going beyond her own tribal language and limits. This work is an important experience at the beginning of her second century. She will be led to closer cooperation with the Reformed Java Christian Church and the Methodist Church (G.M.I.), which work among the Javanese and the Chinese respectively.

The awareness of how to confess the faith in Indonesia today is challenging the churches in Northern Sumatra to promote all efforts for a united witness. In fact, about four years ago they created an instrument for closer cooperation: The regional council of churches in Northern Sumatra is of growing importance in strengthening the cause of Christianity as a whole. Staying close together and advancing together is particularly relevant for the churches over against the Moslems. Whether the Christian-Moslem relationship is one of mutual understanding and tolerance or of mutual self-defense and mistrust is certainly going to affect the life and work of the churches in the future. Unfortunately, the Indonesian Christians have received from the Western missionaries not only the tradition of the faith, but the traditional European attitude toward Moslems prevalent fifty to seventy years ago. But there is no doubt that the Christians' attitude toward their Moslem fellow-citizens should be determined by a readiness for sympathetic understanding and reconciliation. The Indonesian Christians could notice that "there are strong affinities of meaning between the Qu'ran and the Bible, and the common ground provides the surest context for our profound controversies."[24] Kenneth Cragg once preached in a Mosque. He took Surah 11, 61 as his text: "It is He who fashioned you from earth and gave you empire therein: so ask of Him forgiveness and turn to Him penitently. Surely my Lord is nigh." This kind of approach sounds a promising keynote for Christian-Moslem dialogue.[25] The Council of Churches

---

[23] The H.K.B.P. has over 900,000 members and 220 ministers.

[24] *Sermons to Men of Other Faiths and Traditions*, ed. G. H. Anderson (New York, 1966), p. 90.

[25] It is rather regrettable that there are as yet almost no indigenous Christian experts on Islam in the Indonesian Churches.

in Indonesia and its general secretary make serious efforts to imbue the churches in Northern Sumatra with the spirit of perseverance and love in their encounter with the Moslems. In their Christian approach to and social comity with the Moslems lies the key to the future of Christianity as a fellowship of reconciliation in Northern Sumatra in particular, and throughout Indonesia in general.

PRUDENCIO DAMBORIENA is a Roman Catholic priest of the Society of Jesus. From 1936 to 1952 he was a missionary in India, China, and the Philippines, and from 1955 to 1963 he was Dean of the Faculty of Missiology, Gregorian University, Rome. At present he is Associate Professor of Historical Theology at the School of Divinity, St. Louis University, and Chairman of the Department of Ecumenics, Commilas University, Madrid. He also serves as editor for *Pastoral Theology* and for *Corpus Instrumentorum,* Washington, D.C. He is the author of *Fe Catolica e Iglesias y Sectas de la Reforma, El protestantismo en América Latina,* and *Tongues as of Fire: Pentecostalism in Contemporary Christianity.*

5

Prudencio Damboriena, S.J.: **Aspects of the Missionary Crisis in Roman Catholicism**

H ISTORICALLY, PESSIMISM HAS NOT BEEN ONE OF THE VICES OF Roman Catholic missions. Carried by a vision not shared by many others in the West, its missionaries have made their work the most daring enterprise in the Church, and their triumphalism has gone so far as to endorse what seemed lost causes to the rest of the world. As an illustration we may cite the stubbornness with which they have clung for over two decades to the idea of going back to mainland China in order to "resume" the missionary work "interrupted" by the Communist occupation.

In the late fifties, however, the mood began to shift, and today discouragement has gained frightening momentum. Mission stations are being abandoned, and replacements do not arrive to fill the vacancies. The number of vocations in missionary societies has dropped sharply, while periodicals dealing with missions are merged to cover expenses or are simply abandoned. Many men are even afraid to preach the gospel. "We missionaries," says P. de Menasce, "dare not any more to present, with humility and firmness, the grace of God that has been entrusted to us and to share it with others. For fear of paternalism ... we are ashamed of proclaiming the greatest of all our treasures."[1]

---

[1] P. de Menasce, *Permanence et transformation de la mission* (Paris, 1967), p. 173.

Catholic missiology — never a thriving branch in our theology — is at its lowest ebb, and seminary students almost revolt when they see it included in the curriculum. "It is a fact," says Pope Paul VI with typical candor, "that the missionary activity is in crisis, and it would be disloyal to deny it. The idea, the very foundation of *mission* has suffered a kind of degradation in the hands of many Christians."[2] Thus comes to an end among us "the great century of missions" that began as an aftermath of the French revolution and, with a few variations, lasted to the present. Paradoxically, while the Second Vatican Council has stressed as never before the "universality of the Church's mission," we see more and more individuals who, "under the influence of the perspectives of the Council, have dangerously weakened the missionary zeal."[3]

Until recent years the burden of modern Catholic missions was almost entirely in the hands of France, Belgium, Holland, Ireland, and Italy — in that order. The German contribution was never high before the war, although since then its financial support, through such agencies as *Adveniat* and *Misereor,* has reached outstanding proportions. Spain's outlet has been Latin America, and Portugal's, its own overseas dependencies. The North American Church is a recent arrival into the mission field. The United States, whose financial help to missions has been of the first order, has concentrated its activities in the republics south of the border or in territories such as the Philippines or the Pacific Islands, which have been under American influence. The contribution of the Latin American Church, outside its own hemisphere, has been negligible. By missionary families, the Jesuit Order has come first, followed by the Franciscans of the various branches, the Dominicans, the Redemptorists, the Salesians, and those societies (Maryknoll, Divine Word, Paris, Milan, Burgos, and Foreign Mission) which are entirely devoted to mission work. The direct contribution of the diocesan clergy has just begun. The missionary work of women has been almost entirely in the hands of religious sisterhoods and congregations. Catholics have never had anything comparable to the Protestant missionary laity.

Rightly or wrongly, modern Catholic missions have functioned

---

[2] *Osservatore Romano,* May 15, 1966.

[3] G. Phillips, *L'Eglise et son mystere,* I (Paris, 1968), 219.

under the aegis of colonial powers; and they are now suffering the consequences of that. France, Belgium, and even Holland in its Catholic section had issued missionary policies which those who wanted to work in the controlled territories had to obey. The famous *French Protectorate* in China and in the Middle East often became a source of friction between political powers and in many ways hurt the missionary participation of non-French nationals. Belgium in the Congo, Holland in the East Indies, and Portugal in its African possessions, discriminated against missionaries whose loyalty they would not trust. But with the coming of decolonization, the groups mainly rejected (or at least forced to abide by regulations quite different from those prevalent in colonial times) have been precisely those indigenous people recruited in colonial territory — in other words, the most missionary-minded Catholic communities of the Church. To replace them — even on the assumption that there are enough candidates for the task — involves a long and painful process and supposes the building-up at the home base of motivations for missionary commitment different from those of the past, when missions were blended with chauvinistic efforts to raise the economic and cultural standards of the overseas possessions.

No part of the world has been more deeply frustrating to the Christian mission than Asia. While Formosa and, for the present at least, Indonesia are proving receptive to the gospel, and while India fluctuates in its tolerance of evangelism, our missionaries have elsewhere found stern opposition and serious difficulties. They have been expelled from Burma, their movements have been curtailed in Ceylon, and they cannot operate smoothly in the chaotic situations of Laos, Cambodia, Thailand, and Vietnam. Pakistan has always been barren for Christianity. The disenchantment began in China, which was for centuries considered the key to evangelizing Asia. As a substitute, some pioneers — with better intentions than historical and missiological insight — proposed to concentrate on Japan, then on the threshold of its postwar era. But over the years, evangelization there has been more a dream than a reality.

Thus, on the whole, Asia does not appeal to the younger missionary as it did thirty-five years ago. In fact, in certain circles the tendency is to think with K. M. Panikkar that while in China the collapse has been most complete, more generally "the attempt to convert Asia has also definitely failed."

In Africa the outlook is different. While missionaries continue to be greatly handicapped in countries under Islamic dominion, they are welcomed or at least tolerated in other parts of the continent. The bloody interlude in the Congo seems to have been an exception to the rule, and the anti-white movements that certainly persist in many areas are not really aimed at the missionary. Among all foreigners, he is still the most respected. On the other hand, the important Christian pockets (even some powerful minorities) in several Bantu African countries, as well as the number of responsible Christians in public office, seem to guarantee the permanence or even the advance of the Christian faith in Africa.

In the main, however, the role of the missionary around the world is on the decline. The initiative has passed into new hands, and the foreigner is accepted or tolerated according to his willingness to be the servant of all. The change entails sacrifices, and it is still too early to predict how many will be ready to accept them. Once the missionary was a key figure because he was a foreigner, often a member of the ruling European race; now he is a marked man because he belongs to the race that formerly ruled; he is called upon to do "the unspectacular things that others do not want to do." Even his vocation is a perpetual invitation to misunderstanding, when we all know that "to be misunderstood by those you are going to serve is a much harder cross to bear than to be caricatured by the cynics in the homeland you have left behind."[4]

In this situation Catholic missions need a prophetic voice announcing that the present crisis is temporary and that great possibilities are in store for those who with blind faith in the power of the gospel volunteer to do the work of the Lord. Some have referred to the need for another John R. Mott, who even with his oversimplified vision could stir up the spirit of young Americans for "the evangelization of the world in this generation." Certainly such a prophet would be most welcome. But can the issue before us be solved by well-meaning slogans or charismatic leadership, or does it go deeper — into the theological motivations of the mission itself?

---

[4] Douglas Webster, *Yes to Missions* (London, 1966), pp. 25-26.

It is no secret that in the last two decades Roman Catholic theology has experienced an erosion of unprecedented dimensions, covering the whole spectrum of Christian belief from "natural theology" and the rules of "human behavior" to the fundamentals of Christology and the basic doctrines of the Church. As we also know, the revolution began in those countries where formerly the recruitment of missionaries was highest. No wonder, therefore, that its waves have reached the mission field. Regulations (synodic or issued by Propaganda Fide) have suddenly been declared obsolete. Mission policies backed by the experience of generations have been labeled outmoded or opposed to the most progressive theological, pastoral, or liturgical trends of the day. It could not be otherwise with missionaries who as candidates in the West learned to "demythologize" the Bible to the point of making it merely "one of the sacred books of mankind," to harbor serious doubts about the divinity or the resurrection of Christ, and to reinterpret our basic sacramental doctrines or challenge what Roman Catholicism has always held as sacred about the nature and mission of the church. Certain arbitrary interpretations of the documents of the Second Vatican Council (particularly those related to religious freedom, ecumenism, the church in the world, and non-Christian religions) have also done untold harm in the hands of "experts," and no official statements to the contrary, some of them from Pope Paul himself, have prevailed against the contrary views presented in many European or American publications. These reinterpretations have not spared the very nature of the mission of the church. Missionaries and missiologists have been accused of foolishly conceiving the church as "a sanctuary for salvation" or of regarding personal conversion as its aim when, "in the light of the Council it is becoming more and more difficult to hold that Christians have a better and easier chance to be saved than non-Christians."[5]

The results of this irruption (which reminds Protestants of their own conflicts of forty years ago at the time of the *Laymen's Commission* and William Ernest Hocking's *Re-Thinking Missions*) can be easily gauged — the disenchantment and often withdrawal of mature missionaries, confusion and doubts among

---

[5] W. B. Frazier in *The Church as Sign*, ed. W. J. Richardson (New York, 1968), p. 6.

the national clergy, and scandal among the faithful, whose simple faith has been shaken by the novelties and contradictions. The same principles have helped to establish a new missionary program based on social and secular objectives (the dream of the Peace Corps) or made up of "prophetism," "horizontal diakonia," "missionary presence," and "involvement in the world," while giving up the old methods of evangelizing and conversion on the grounds that "non-Christians do not need membership in the visible Church in order to be saved; they do not need the Church to arrive at a deeper awareness of the saving mystery by which they are continually embraced."[6]

The missionary malaise is, to a great extent at least, a reflection of a deeper illness affecting the whole body of the church. I cannot avoid feeling that certain theologians have taken positions and issued principles which carried to their logical end would simply mean death for the mission of the church. One of those principles concerns the exclusiveness of Christianity in regard to all other religions, and consequently the need for Christian faith and conversion to attain salvation. If these truths are doubted or virtually denied, the missionary work of the church loses its meaning. For twenty centuries they have been the foundation of Christian missions. To shake them is inevitably to cause the whole edifice of mission to crumble. Their practical denial explains to a great extent the missionary decline — if not catastrophe — we are witnessing. I allude, of course, to the theory of *anonymous Christians.*

The two key words to describe the relationship between Christian revelation and non-Christian religions have been "discontinuity" and "continuity," or rather, "fulfillment." Following a long-honored tradition going back to the *Logos spermatikos* school of the early centuries, Catholic theology has clearly favored the theory of *fulfillment,* which, supplemented with the Augustinian dictum *facienti quod est in se Deus non denegat gratiam* (God does not deny his grace to those who do what they can on their part), has attempted to explain the bottomless mystery of predestination and the possibility of salvation for those who die outside the fold of the visible church or have not even come to the explicit knowledge of the gospel. The theory, although dormant during the Middle Ages (Thomas

---

[6] *Ibid.*

Aquinas was rather short-sighted about the salvation of pagans), was unearthed, discussed, and developed during and after the Age of the Discovery. Few missionaries and theologians went so far as the China Jesuits in their appraisal of Asian religions, but the original optimistic view was never abandoned. With the resumption of modern missions — and in spite of the degrading evaluations of pagan beliefs and practices made by certain Catholic missionaries — the old attitude has been resumed, as shown for instance in the works of three contemporary writers: L. Caperan's *Le problème du salut des infidèles;* Ch. Journet's *L'Eglise du Verbe Incarné;* and R. Lombardi's *The Salvation of the Unbeliever.*[7]

The way was therefore prepared to resume a discussion as old as the Christian mission itself. The parallel controversies of Barth, Brunner, and Kraemer had made little impact upon the thinking of Catholic missiologists. But other elements entered the scene. I have already mentioned such ideas as ecumenism and religious tolerance, which through misinterpretation by certain theologians have sown confusion among missionaries. Decolonialization, the loss of Asia, and the uncertainties of the church's work in parts of Africa, inclined some to despair of the possibility of evangelizing the whole *oikoumene* — a feeling deepened by the resurgence of the great Asian religions and by the bitter accusations of national leaders that the missionaries had mistreated members of the indigenous faiths. Word began to spread about the need of a radical shift in the aim of missions. If religious pluralism is according to the will of God, Christians ought to be satisfied with being a "little flock" surrounded by secularism and ready to witness to the Lord not through preaching but simply through their presence in the world:

> The real crisis of mission today is the Church's failure to function consistently in the world as a relevant sign of God's redeeming love, a failure to be present and active in today's version of the human conflict, a hesitancy to take sides, a refusal to speak out. The failure of the Christian

---

[7] L. Caperan, *Le Problème du salut des infidèles* (Toulouse, 1934)— updated by the author with a more recent study: *L'appel non-chretien au salut* (Paris, 1961); Ch. Journet, *L'Eglise du Verbe Incarné*, II (Bruges, 1961); R. Lombardi, *The Salvation of the Unbeliever* (Westminster, Md., 1956).

mission today is not a failure to convert the world, but the failure to convert the Church to the world.[8]

An atmosphere of pessimism about the power of the gospel, and the tendency to make Christianity easy to contemporaries have been a perpetual temptation in the church. Origen and his followers advocated preaching forgiveness after death for those who had died unrepentant. Cardinal Billot equated the pagans — so far as knowledge of God is concerned — to infants dying before the age of reason. Their modern counterparts have preferred to raise non-Christian religions, as instruments of salvation, to the level of Christian revelation.

The theory of an "anonymous Christianity" and of "anonymous Christians" owes its origins to Karl Rahner and was thrown onto the theological market in the late fifties. Knowing that it was not backed either by Scripture or by tradition, the German theologian begged his readers and listeners to judge his "Catholic dogmatic interpretation" according to "the weight of the reasons we can adduce."[9]

On principle at least, Rahner admits that Christianity is the absolute religion. Because of the Incarnation, it holds a unique place between God and man, continues its presence in the church, and entrusts her with the commission of preaching the gospel to the whole world. "Christianity understands itself as the absolute religion, instituted for all men, which cannot recognize any other religion besides itself as of equal right. This proposition is self-evident and basic for Christianity's understanding of itself."[10] But at the same time, Rahner believes that Catholic tradition has overstressed the need for salvation and developed a theology of the cross that does not fit within the framework of a forgiving God who meets the sinner in ways which often defy our human understanding. Rejecting the Augustinian concept of the Two Cities, he considers the world as "the divinized ground of man," driven by the "dynamism of grace under a supernatural, saving providence of God." "Salvation-history," he adds, "takes place right in the midst of ordinary history. Man works out his salvation or damnation in

---

[8] Frazier, p. 7.

[9] K. Rahner, *Theological Investigations*, V (Baltimore, 1966), 117.

[10] *Ibid.*, p. 118. See also Rahner's *Grace and Freedom* (New York, 1969), p. 82.

everything he does. ... The history of the world ... is ... [also] the pre-history of Christ."[11] Rahner also accepts man's obligation to listen to the message of the gospel, but restricts it to the historical moment in which the message is proposed to him in such a way that it cannot be rejected by any sensible person. Since, however, such is not the case with billions of pagans in mission lands (not much is said of the millions of agnostics and deists in the "Christian West") Rahner intends to facilitate their lot by following "theological reflection." In this "divinized" world of ours God wants the salvation of all men. Moreover, this

> is a salvation really *intended* for all those millions and mil-
> lions of men who lived perhaps a million years before
> Christ — and also for those who lived after Christ — in
> nations, cultures and epochs of a very wide range which
> were still completely shut off from the viewpoint of those
> living in the light of the New Testament.[12]

Consequently — and this is Rahner's jump into the void — it is impossible

> to think that this offer of supernatural, divinizing grace
> made to all men on account of the universal salvific pur-
> pose of God, should in general (prescinding from the rela-
> tively few exceptions) remain ineffective in most cases on
> account of the personal guilt of the individual. ... As far as
> the gospel is concerned, we have no really conclusive rea-
> son for thinking so pessimistically of men. ... Christ and
> his salvation are not simply one of two possibilities offering
> themselves to man's free choice. ... In Christ God not only
> gives the *possibility* ... but actual salvation. ... Hence we
> have every right to suppose ... that in a great many cases
> at least, grace gains victory in man's free acceptance
> of it. ...[13]

Therefore, if, on the one hand, God's universal saving will holds a power which practically forces man to accept his grace, and, on the other, the majority of mankind professes religions dif-

---

[11] *Theological Investigations*, V, 105, 99, 114.
[12] *Ibid.*, p. 123.
[13] *Ibid.*, pp. 123-24.

ferent from Judaism and Christianity, the obvious next step will be to raise those faiths to be legal channels of salvation:

> A lawful religion means here an institutional religion whose "use" by man at a certain period can be regarded on the whole as a positive means of gaining the right relationship to God and thus for the attaining of salvation, a means which is therefore positively included in God's plan of salvation.[14]

Rahner is not specific about which religions are included in this category, although his few references aim at the higher Asian religions. Of one thing we should be certain: "Taken in its totality... [such religion] is the way in which man encounters the natural divine law according to God's will" (p. 129), and consequently his true way to salvation.

Hence results an important missiological conclusion: "Christianity does not simply confront the member of an extra-Christian religion as a mere non-Christian but as someone who can and must already be regarded in this or that respect as an anonymous Christian" (p. 131). Such a man, because of the grace he has experienced in himself, "has already been given revelation in a true sense even before he has been affected by missionary preaching from without" (*ibid.*). On this hypothesis the whole missionary strategy of the past must be reversed. What the messenger of the gospel brings to the non-Christian

> is not... the proclamation of something as yet absolutely unknown... but the expression in objective concepts of something which that person has already attained or could already have attained in the depth of his rational existence. ... In the last analysis, the proclamation of the gospel does not simply turn someone absolutely abandoned by God and Christ into a Christian, but turns an anonymous Christian into someone who also knows about his Christian belief in the depths of his grace-endowed being by objective reflection and by the profession of faith which is given social form in the church. (*Ibid.*)

Thus the necessity of missions does not derive from man's worry about his personal salvation. This is already assured in paganism.

---

[14] *Ibid.,* p. 125.

It derives from a positive mission of God and Christ and is founded on the incarnational structure which is unique to Christianity and demands that the supernatural gift which God has made of himself in the grace of the Spirit might show forth its historical and sociological character. (Translation mine.)[15]

Clearly, Rahner's departure from traditional missiology is radical. Overnight those non-Christian religions that were either woefully despised or at most tolerated by missionaries and theologians, have become "legal instruments" of salvation. The aim of missions, which formerly included as an essential aspect the salvation of the individual, is now identified with a vague work of explicating religious convictions already professed by non-Christians — convictions, incidentally, which per se would be more than sufficient to attain their salvation. Thus the "missionary obligation of the Church" loses its main appeal for men and women who, driven by the noble ideal of the christianization of mankind, volunteered for missions.

As was to be feared, Rahner's disciples have refused to stop at his conclusions. R. Schlette and Hans Küng speak of non-Christian religions as "normal" and "ordinary" means of salvation, and see "God's providential design" in the religious plurality of the world. "Non-Christian religions can be considered institutions showing in a visible and historical manner the salvific will of God to those who are outside the special history of salvation."[16] Catholics, Küng warns us, should also give up the old saying that "outside the Church there is no salvation." The idea makes it extremely difficult for missionaries to preach the gospel and "is rightly rejected by thinking non-Christians as a piece of purely theological construction and speculation." Instead, "as against the *extraordinary way of salvation which is the Church,* the world-religions can be called the *ordinary way* of salvation for non-Christian humanity" (italics mine).[17] For Raymond Paniker "every authentic religion has existentially the function of leading man to God"; religions are "as different rays of one and

---

[15] Rahner, ed., *Handbuch der Pastoraltheologie* (Fribourg, 1966), Band II/2.

[16] R. Schlette, *Towards a Theology of Religions* (London, 1966), p. 67.

[17] Hans Küng in *Christian Revelation and World Religions,* ed. J. Neuner (London, 1965), pp. 36, 51-52.

the same light" or as "rivers flowing to the same sea" or "become different ways that men take to reach their goal, since in fact it is the End which really inspires, attracts and produces everything that has life on earth."[18] Others will probably follow with even more extremist conclusions.

The initial reaction among missionaries and missiologists to these theories was shock and surprise. Their promoters, most of them inexperienced in missionary matters, had dared to meddle in problems requiring a direct acquaintance with non-Christian religions and the actual evangelistic work of missions. The opposition took various forms. At the Second Vatican Council many bishops denounced the theories as proposals that would choke all future missionary vocations. The same accusation was made by Superior Generals in important missionary orders (Jesuits, Dominicans, Missionaries of the Holy Spirit, Paris and Burgos Missionary Societies, and others) after they realized in their own ranks the disastrous effects of accepting them. The response of veterans in the mission field was likewise negative and at times bitter and disappointed: the proposals went against the ideals they had cherished and worked for in their lives, seemed unrealistic when tested against the realities of missionary experience, and constituted a slap in the face to most intelligent pagans, who did not want in the least to be called anonymous Christians but were proud of their own non-Christian religious heritage. Likewise, responsible missiologists gave it a cool reception: the theories lacked the minimum requisites to be accepted as a scientific working hypothesis, and on the practical level would only add to the already existing confusion regarding certain aspects of the missionary enterprise. The best commentaries to the documents of the Second Vatican Council preferred to reject the notion of an anonymous Christianity.

The heaviest barrage has come from professional theologians. Well-known figures like De Lubac, Phillips, Liegé, Journet, Durwell, von Balthasar, De Letter, Grasso, and Danielou have taken a strong position against the innovation. Biblically they find it groundless. The theory can be defended only by twisting the obvious meaning of paganism in the Old and New Testaments and by taking various phrases out of context. Neither can the most optimistic tradition of the Fathers or the history of mis-

---

[18] R. Paniker, *Religion y religiónes* (Madrid, 1963), p. 162.

sions in their rapprochement to non-Christian religions provide solid ground for their interpretation. It never occurred to them to lower Christianity to the level of non-Christian religions or to make of these religions legal channels of salvation. From the viewpoint of systematic theology, the theory has been found wanting in many ways: the "divinization" of the world as a result of Christ's redemption has been grossly exaggerated; there is a regrettable confusion between the *offer* of salvation made to each one of us by Christ, and our totally free *acceptance* of it; serious-minded scholars should not play with words like "ordinary" or "normal" when these expressions have a definite meaning in Christian tradition; Rahner and his disciples have woefully neglected the radical changes (the true *metanoia* of the gospel) involved in the process from unbelief to faith, while failing also to stress the theology of the cross as inseparable from the life of the Christian. Certain responsible church authorities have deemed it necessary to add their warning. The head of the Congregation on Missions denounced the departure as without foundation in the documents of the Council and extremely dangerous to the evangelization of the world. And prominent members of the Secretariat for non-Christians see in it an attempt to endanger — if not in words, at least in practice — the absoluteness of Christian revelation.

The middle of the road position on the matter seems to be that adopted by De Lubac and von Balthasar. They would accept the concept of "anonymous Christians" — provided it were not exposed to so many abuses — if this referred only to men and women (in numbers totally unknown to us) who, through different channels, "have received the light that has come from the Gospel or through some secret action of the Spirit of Christ." But what these authors consider a paralogism is to speak of an "anonymous Christianity" — or "implicit Christianity" — diffused in the hearts of all men in such a way that the only role of apostolic preaching is to make it pass, without any intrinsic change, to the explicit state, as if the revelation of Christ were no more than the unveiling of something that already existed there. "When Saint Augustine," adds De Lubac,

> saw the grace of Christ working in the holy men of the history of Israel who, consequently, even before the Incarnation, "belonged already to the economy of grace and

85

not to that of law," he did not confuse those two economies, as if the Old Testament, considered in history, contained already in his time the whole reality of the New Testament. How much less is it possible to consider pagan humanity, in the forms of worship it has elaborated, as a Church that does not know herself. This thesis cannot be maintained except by mixing up two problems which we must begin to delineate with all possible clarity: the problem of truth and of the salvific efficaciousness of a teaching and of a religious organism, and that of the personal appropriation of salvation — the latter being possible, with divine grace, to any individual, and treated in theology under the heading of *the salvation of the unbeliever.* The opposite reasoning means the neglect of the real history of mankind in order to let ourselves be guided by a priori ideas which suppose in practice the equivalence of different religions, their common relativity and common aptitude to play the role of *instruments* and *ways of salvation.* . . . Finally, such a theory — and this is extremely serious — ignores not only the idea, but even the reality of the change (*metanoia*) produced by the gospel, a change by which man is profoundly transformed in his heart and conscience, and it forgets the profoundly existential character of Christian revelation. . . . In the opposite case there would be no reason for some men to carry the name of "Christian" since their own *anonymity* would so easily justify itself.[19] (Translation mine; italics mine.)

Now in the same paragraph the author states that the position he criticizes here "does not in any way correspond to the idea of revelation taught by the Second Vatican Council." "This enlightening distinction," concludes von Balthasar,

. . . seems to satisfy our present needs: the certainty, on the one hand, that the Christian preacher does not enter a domain devoid of grace, since Christ died for everyone, and the urgent need on the other, to testify by our whole

---

[19] Henri de Lubac, *Paradoxe et mystère de l'Eglise* (Paris, 1967), pp. 154-56.

existence to the unique grace that God has bestowed on us in his Son.[20] (Translation mine.)

Such is the state of the controversy in our days. But its consequences are far from exhausted. While the best Catholic theology has offered opposite answers to the problem, a great many individuals, won over by its simplistic appeal, continue to visualize the work of missions under this new light and advocate radical changes in the aim and strategy of missions. Only time will tell us if their net outcome redounds to the glory of God and the salvation of redeemed mankind.

---

[20] Urs von Balthasar, *Cordula*, p. 121.

HAROLD LINDSELL, ordained in the Southern Baptist Convention, graduated from Wheaton College, earned his Ph.D. in history from New York University, and in 1964 received a D.D. from Fuller Theological Seminary. He taught church history and missions at Columbia Bible College in South Carolina from 1942 to 1944, and at Northern Baptist Theological Seminary in Chicago from 1944 to 1947. From 1947 to 1964 he served as the Vice President and Dean of Faculty of Fuller Theological Seminary. He was the associate editor of *Christianity Today* from 1964 to 1967 and is now editor of that magazine. His many publications include *Christian Philosophy of Missions, Missionary Principles and Practice,* and *Christianity and the Cults,* and he edited *The Church's Worldwide Mission.*

6

Harold Lindsell: The Evangelical Missions: The Home Base

To forecast the future for evangelical churches we must immediately answer two questions: What churches are we talking about? and What do we conceive the world mission of evangelical churches to be?

The evangelical churches constitute a mixed bag. Most of the denominations in the World and National Councils of Churches cannot be said to be distinctively evangelical if we mean by this having a thoroughgoing commitment to historic orthodoxy. But there are a multitude of local congregations within these denominations that are evangelical in their theology, and these must be listed among the evangelicals.

A number of denominations unrelated to ecumenical organizations are also generally said to be evangelical: the Southern Baptist Convention and The Lutheran Church-Missouri Synod are examples. There are many others around the world.

The churches and denominations in the National Association of Evangelicals must be included. So must the faith missionary societies and the independent and Bible churches that support them, and the mission churches overseas.

Finally we must include all individuals who are evangelical whatever their church ties, those people who are members of local congregations that are theologically unorthodox but who, for one reason or another, maintain their membership in such churches. It surely would have to include some Roman Catholics.

The second question is even more important than the first, for how one defines the Christian world mission makes all the difference. Certainly the church's mission as spelled out by the World Council of Churches at Uppsala is profoundly dissimilar to that articulated by evangelicals. How someone like John Bennett of Union Theological Seminary defines the church's mission is likewise far removed from what evangelicals espouse. The correctness of evangelical belief about the church's mission need not be debated here. But the content of that belief should be stated.

Evangelicals have firm opinions about proclamation and service — that is, kerygma and *diakonia*. Despite repeated attacks by liberals, they do assent to, and are involved in, social action. However, they do not think that the church *qua* church should make pronouncements about or become immersed in economic and political matters. The church is not competent in these areas and has no biblical mandate from God to make official statements. Individual Christians, as members of Caesar's kingdom as well as of God's kingdom, should be involved in political and economic affairs insofar as they are competent and have opportunity. But the church as church should engage in works of mercy, including such things as relief for the poor, help for the underprivileged, medical aid for the sick, and education for the illiterate.

The mission of the church is preeminently spiritual — that is, its major concern revolves around the nonmaterial aspects of life. Of necessity it carries out its mission in the material realm. But service (*diakonia*), though certainly energized by the spiritual outlook of life, is not equal with but secondary to the proclamation of the gospel. Kerygma and service are true yokefellows, but even as in marriage the headship belongs to the husband, so kerygma has ordered priority over service. The implications of this relationship must be examined afresh in every age, and continuing research is required to maintain in practice what is believed in principle.

Claiming priority for proclamation is not the whole story. The mission of the church is to evangelize the world, that is, to preach the gospel to every creature. Not all will be saved. The church's business is to be God's agent as he calls out for himself a people for his name. The present world is irretrievably doomed. It must and it will pass away. Therefore history has a *terminus ad quem*. Just as it had a beginning, so also does it have an end. The evangelical looks for a new heaven and a new earth, for the old heaven and the old earth must pass away. The world system is doomed also. The kings and nations of this planet must yield to Jesus Christ and his kingdom. This is a radical and revolutionary viewpoint that will be fulfilled only when God breaks into history once more via the second advent of his Son to consummate what he began in his plan of the ages before creation began.

Evangelicals are tied to two polarities that appear at times to be irreconcilable. One is that the church is commanded to evangelize the world and that its failure to do so will thwart the purpose of God. The other is that God has promised to fulfill inexorably his own purpose. Strangely enough command and promise are both true. The church must act in obedience and at the same time rest in the conviction that Scripture has prophesied that this gospel carries with it everlasting sanctions. There is a heaven to gain and a hell to shun. God freely offers life to those who respond and leaves in death those who spurn his gracious offer. They are simply confirmed forever in what they now are and what they refuse to give up. To be in hell is to be without God. And men who spurn the gospel are already in that relationship.

What then is the future of the Christian world mission for the evangelical churches?

All churches are in ferment, all are under attack from within as well as from without. The tide seems to be ebbing. Evangelical churches are not immune to these attacks, and their future viability depends on how they respond in the next decade or two. The nonevangelical churches are far along the road to irrelevance, secularism, apostasy, and possibly extinction. Evangelical churches are not safe, and while they have not yet capitulated they are in danger of doing so. Where then is the erosion taking place?

Affluence, in common with most of the churches, has overtaken evangelicals. They have never had it so good. The quest for material goods has deeply infected both clergy and laity. Prosperity has not only fulfilled former expectations, it has whetted appetites for more things and has raised the level of expectation. That which was formerly regarded as luxury now has become necessity. The mind-set of evangelicals has been turned

91

very subtly from its focus on the world to come to this present world. Yet, since their senses have been dulled in the process, most evangelicals are not aware of the change. They have changed but they don't know it. Perhaps only a severe economic depression will awaken them.

Social action has become a driving force among evangelicals and could easily quench their zeal for evangelism both at home and abroad. At a time when great sums of money are readily available, the overseas task force has not grown appreciably. Overseas outreach has peaked. It is not unrealistic to suppose that unless there is some kind of renascence, evangelical outreach, like that of the ecumenical forces, will atrophy. But the trend toward greater social involvement is not the cause for the declining interest in evangelism (not to be identified with social action). On the contrary, the trend toward social involvement has resulted from the decreased interest in evangelism. When a vacuum was created by the decline of evangelism, something had to take its place. Not that there is no place for social action. But when the proper relationship and the correct balance are changed, then social action gains an ascendancy that does not belong to it.

Evangelicals are currently afflicted by the relativism of situation ethics. As a consequence the definition of worldliness has shifted considerably. The binding nature of the law of God has often been compromised by an ill-defined and personally interpreted law of love divorced from the Ten Commandments. Whereas lying, for example, has traditionally been regarded as an absolute, it is now treated relatively by many evangelicals. It is superseded by the law of love. Therefore, under the guise of love, lying is sometimes justified, even though the commandment is thereby nullified. So also fornication is not sin so long as it is meaningful and involves concern and love. The fact that it breaches the commandment of God is quite incidental. This relativism in ethics not only cheapens the law of God with respect to personal conduct, it also cheapens the command of God with respect to the Great Commission. When the absolutes of God are suspended in one area, they languish in other areas as well. Consequently the zeal to fulfill the missionary mandate both with respect to candidates and support has abated and probably will weaken even more severely in the days ahead.

But despite the general weakening of missionary concern, there are evidences that the Spirit is breaking out through new channels. The activities of Campus Crusade for Christ, with its almost two thousand workers on college campuses around the world, are one illustration. The continued power of the evangelistic outreach of Billy Graham is another. This is especially true of the coast-to-coast television presentations of his local crusades. The progress of the Pentecostals in Latin America is another. Continuing revival in Ruanda is still another.

A further illustration of spiritual vitality is found in the recent congresses on evangelism. Under the auspices of *Christianity Today* and the Billy Graham Evangelistic Association, the first World Congress convened in Berlin in 1966. Nothing like this had been held since the great missionary conference at Edinburgh in 1910. The delegates came from churches both in and out of the Ecumenical Movement. Almost every geographical area of the world was represented. People from every major denomination, including Pentecostals, were present. It was undoubtedly the most truly ecumenical Protestant gathering in more than fifty years. A solid theological foundation for evangelism was advanced in Berlin. The value of Berlin was not simply that such a congress was convened, significant as that was, but that it triggered regional congresses around the world. In 1968 evangelicals of East Asia and the South Pacific met in Singapore. Underwritten by the Billy Graham organization and sparked by the brilliant leadership of Stan Mooneyham, who was to become president of World Vision shortly thereafter, evangelicals from as far north as Korea and as far south as Australia and New Zealand convened to discuss evangelism and spark a renewed interest in the outreach of the church. Again and again the note was struck that the decadence of Western white Christianity was a challenge to the East to fill the gap and finish the job of worldwide evangelization.

In September, 1969, the U. S. Congress on Evangelism met in Minneapolis. With more than 4500 delegates from all over the United States, it was surely the most broadly based Protestant gathering in the country, apart from mass evangelistic crusades. Evangelicals from almost every large and small denomination were present. *Time* magazine declared that evangelical Christianity had come of age by harnessing evangelism and social outreach into a workable combination.

In November of the same year the Latin America Congress on Evangelism met in Bogotá, Colombia. Almost a thousand delegates attended. Underwritten by the Billy Graham Evangelistic Association, it brought new life to evangelism in a continent dominated by the Roman Catholic Church for centuries.

A congress met in Africa and another in Canada in 1970. Still another congress is planned for Mexico City. And as this is being written, plans are under way for another world congress that would bring together 2500 to 3000 evangelicals from around the globe.

Any movement away from theological orthodoxy is bound to have a substantial impact on the future of the evangelical world mission. History affords us illustrations of this. What usually happens is that the mission of the church is redefined. The direction in which the churches were moving is shifted. The old views are challenged or are reinterpreted so that substantive changes occur. Missionary concern diminishes until finally the spark goes and the dynamic is lost. This deterioration is not necessarily rapid. Some missionaries and laymen may continue to bear witness faithfully, hoping to stem the tide and reverse the trend. But this reversal rarely, if ever, happens. Sloth and backsliding increase and spiritual decay results.

In addition to destructive forces at work within the churches, certain changes on the world scene add immeasurably to the uncertainty of the times for all. Evangelicals, along with others, have been caught unprepared by the population, transportation, communications, and knowledge explosions, and have either failed to respond to these challenges or simply do not know how to respond. Evangelicals, like other people, have tended to cling to the old patterns, to opt for the status quo, because they fear change and dread what they do not fully understand. Such a reaction by men outside the church is not astonishing, but for evangelicals to react this way is disconcerting, since they profess certainty about God's plan in history, are warned in Scripture against surprise, and are told to discern the signs of the times. The path of least resistance is to retreat behind a barricade and become otherworldly. It is to run away from the challenges of the hour, to cop out on history. Both in and out of the churches, some young people have found life too much for them and have abdicated. Evangelicals cannot escape the fact that this poses a great danger for them: to isolate themselves in self-contained units, happy to talk to themselves and unwilling to risk the dangers of confrontation with the world and the items on the world's agenda.

In the present situation any hope for a breakthrough and dynamic advance by the evangelical churches is minimal. Given present trends, all we can anticipate is a continuation of the current evangelical pace, if not a substantial slowdown. Never have so many people needed evangelization; never have the social, economic, and political problems been graver; never has man had available to him instruments that could eliminate the whole human race; never has man possessed so much knowledge or had in his grasp so many solutions to problems that could make earth the kind of place God intended it to be. But never has man been further from the fulfillment of this ideal because of his corrupted nature, his greed and pride, his determination to act autonomously without reference to his Creator or his Creator's laws. Perhaps the greatest reason of all for pessimism about the future of evangelical churches is their moribund spiritual condition.

If theological liberalism is bankrupt and if it has signally failed in its effort to redeem society, evangelicals have not succeeded in halting the spiritual decline in America and around the world. Sweden, Germany, Denmark, and Great Britain once enjoyed a vital and dynamic Christianity. Now all these countries are in a state of sad spiritual disarray. Yet in none of them have the evangelical forces rallied to stem the tide or reverse it. The same is true in the United States. Evangelicals constantly bemoan the decay of Christianity, and they pinpoint with amazing accuracy the rising tide of crime, immorality, lawlessness, disorder, and theological apostasy. But they have not been able to halt the decline. They have often enshrined their right doctrine on a pedestal, and in so doing have failed to grasp one weighty lesson that history teaches all who read its pages. Those whose theology is aberrant must of necessity fail. The history of liberalism proves this. But while those whose theology is biblical need not fail, they can and they do fail when they become spiritually sterile. In general (there are always minor exceptions) evangelicalism has become sterile. It has lost its dynamic. It is on the defensive. It has cloistered itself from the world and thus has not been able to evangelize it. To shoot arrows at the enemy from behind impenetrable barricades assures the safety of those who wield the bows. But it never gets the job done. Unless and until evangelicals emerge from their barricades and take the gospel to people in face to face confrontation, there is no hope that they will win battles or reverse trends.

The life and ministry of John Wesley pointedly illustrates what is needed and what is missing among evangelical churches. Wesley went where the need existed. He risked life and limb to wrestle eyeball to eyeball with those who needed Jesus Christ. So did Whitefield. They suffered wounds in the process, but they also experienced victory. The great Evangelical Awakening in England turned the tide, and righteousness won the day. Wesley's power can be traced to that Aldersgate experience where his theological orthodoxy was set on fire by the power of the Holy Spirit.

Evangelicalism's plight today lies in its failure to experience the fullness and power of the Holy Spirit. And until it does, its orthodoxy is dead and its future dark. The history of renewal shows that the deepest and most significant changes are wrought under the impulse and dynamic power of a few Spirit-filled people. The key figures who sparked the Reformation number less than a dozen. The Evangelical Awakening of the eighteenth century was spearheaded by half a dozen men. God chose a single man to inspire and lead his people out of Egypt. Jesus Christ selected eleven men to be responsible for the advance of the infant church after Pentecost. In a real sense the man of this age has been Billy Graham. But somehow the fire from the altar has not yet ignited as it has at other times in the history of the church. Perhaps the key to the problem lies in the sovereignty of God, whose plans elude us and whose ways are not our ways. We can predict confidently, however, that unless there is renewal among the evangelical churches, renewal such as we have not experienced for many decades, they will become a smaller and smaller minority, exerting less and less influence on the culture that surrounds them. The next decade may spell the difference between a resurgent evangelicalism and a declining, moribund community of orthodox but powerless believers.

ARTHUR F. GLASSER attended Cornell University, the Moody Bible Institute, Faith Theological Seminary, and Union Theological Seminary in New York, where he earned his S.T.M. in 1970. Previously he was awarded a D.D. by Covenant College and Theological Seminary, St. Louis. After a Navy chaplaincy during World War II, he served as a missionary with the China Inland Mission. He taught at Columbia Bible College and thereupon became an administrator for the CIM-Overseas Missionary Fellowship for North America. Since 1970 he has been Associate Dean and Associate Professor of Missions at the Graduate School of World Missions and Institute of Church Growth at Fuller Theological Seminary, Pasadena, California. Besides various articles, he has written *And Some Believe* and (with Eric F. Fife) *Missions in Crisis*. An ordained minister of the Reformed Presbyterian Church (Evangelical Synod), he serves on the boards of a number of evangelical mission societies.

7

Arthur F. Glasser: # The Evangelicals: World Outreach

IN HIS ESSAY, DR. LINDSELL HAS MAINLY DESCRIBED CERTAIN DOMI-nant characteristics of the evangelical home base in America at the beginning of the seventies. I should like to follow this with an expanded exploration of evangelical outreach across the world.

EVENT ORIENTATION

During the closing days of 1970, the ninth triennial Inter-Varsity Christian Fellowship (IVCF) missionary convention for students was held at the University of Illinois in Urbana. Over 12,000 students attended (up 25 percent from 1967). For four and a half days they engaged in small-group Bible study, prayed, sang, attended lectures on contemporary issues, and listened to the exposition of Scripture. All activities focused on the theme "World Evangelism." In one offering the students gave $72,000 (plus $18,000 in pledges) for student evangelism overseas. After a solemn celebration of the Lord's Supper, they slowly left the assembly singing the popular Roman Catholic song: "We are one in the Spirit, we are one in the Lord.... And we pray that all unity may one day be restored.... And they'll know we are Christians by our love...."

Approximately 400 missionaries were there also, representing almost a hundred Protestant societies. The very existence of these organizations could be attributed in large measure to the concern of Christian students in earlier decades, from the 1806

Haystack Prayer Meeting (behind Williams College) onward. No missionary disagreed with David Howard, the keynote speaker, when he pressed home the obligation: "Today we dare not ignore the burning issues of race relations, economic injustice, and imperialism." But they rejoiced when he clearly affirmed: "By the same token, we dare not ignore God's eternal commands to make the Gospel of Jesus Christ available to all mankind." Later, when hundreds of students arose to commit themselves to Christ and his Lordship, these missionaries could not but recall their own conversion years before. When the call was issued to participate with Christ in the worldwide mission of his church, it was apparent from the thousands who responded that the NOW generation was anything but indifferent to his will.

This convention was but one contemporary reenactment of the distinctives of the eighteenth-century Evangelical Awakening, with its stress on personal conversion, the inward witness of the Spirit, the obligation to personal holiness, and the call to evangelism and service. During the same period, Campus Crusade for Christ, a parallel student organization, was conducting a series of regional gatherings with the same distinctives. Is this the new wine of which Christ spoke? Suffice it to say, the guardians of the evangelical religious establishment (churchmen and missionaries) cannot but wonder whether their organizational wineskins can contain such newness of life. On the other hand, many of the older main-line missionary operations appear quite indifferent to the problem. Despite the fact that United Presbyterians had more students at Urbana than any other denomination, they hope to reduce their foreign personnel by another third in the next two years. In other churches programs are being curtailed and personnel reassigned. The official line is that the era is "post-Christian" and "the day of missions is drawing to an end." Naturally such pessimism does not stimulate giving nor encourage most young Christians to offer themselves for service. Among other things it reveals a lack of "event" orientation, which leads to an inability to appreciate the significance of today's vital "happenings" (such as Urbana '70, the Billy Graham crusades, congresses on evangelism, unstructured student movements, and many others). Much of the current negativism among church leaders has arisen from either a toleration of theological confusion or an apparent unwillingness to take these events as God intended them to be taken. One can easily miss the way, philosophize about events, and then dismiss them. But the focus of God's dealings with men is the event. As Eugene A. Nida has succinctly stated: "The ultimate reality apprehendable by man is not to be found in isolated qualities, but in behavior relationships expressed by concrete actions in the realm of time."[1]

Evangelicals firmly believe that many of the Christward movements in our day should be regarded as "events," calling the church back into focus. Student movements are particularly significant. Students are demonstrating in hundreds of separate locations that their encounter with God through Jesus Christ can be transformed into a pattern for mission. Principles can be abstracted from their gatherings, and these principles can in turn be fed into people groupings in other places to produce similar "happenings." God is seeking a succession of encounters between himself and his creatures. In part the Bible is the record of a theology of events. This is why it grips the mind, stirs the imagination, and generates faith. "The same Lord is Lord of all, and bestows his riches upon all who call upon him" (Rom. 10:12). Eventually, movements are generated which extend the work of his Spirit among men. All this can be lost on those intellectually conditioned to reject the evidence that fails to conform to their presuppositions.

At this point we need to remind ourselves that the evangelical movement is not to be taken as confined to certain ecclesiastical or missionary structures. To do so leads to the mistaken conclusion that evangelicalism is to be equated with separatist denominations and their parochial missionary structures. To avoid this misconception, many evangelicals reject the "fundamentalist" label, which is too easily construed in the public mind as a rabid sectarianism, capable only of furnishing recruits for the lunatic fringe. The evangelical movement, rightly understood, represents a tenacious insistence on the essential and central dogmas of historic, biblical Christianity. It is no ism of recent vintage. True, it has an ambivalent character. Its thrust ranges from the reform movement within existing church structures to separation from the unreformable when it appears that the truth of the gospel cannot be maintained in any other way. Wesley

---

[1] *Message and Mission* (New York, 1960), p. 224.

had no intention of leaving the Church of England. His over-riding concern was to call Anglicans to repentance and faith in Christ, so that the ancient marks of devotion to "apostolic teaching and fellowship, to the breaking of bread and prayers" (Acts 2:42) might once again be manifest in their midst. When his reform movement was resisted by the clergy, a split was inevitable. Down through the history of the church few reform movements have been contained within old structures. Their new dynamisms necessitated new structures. Kenneth Scott Latourette heralded the proliferation of reform movements and the new missionary structures they sometimes produce as "signs of vitality." When they cease to appear, faith is "somnolent or moribund." The more diversity in Protestant operations, he reasoned, the greater the overall response and the deeper the roots of indigenous forms of Christianity throughout the world.[2]

Of course, leaders of the ecclesiastical establishment might reason differently. An older case in point would be the Irish Peregrini. At this distance they sound like evangelicals! For more than 400 years (A.D. 500-950) they preached the gospel throughout Europe. Latourette observes that "they were an irritation to the Churchmen on the Continent, for they did not readily fit into the diocesan pattern."[3]

POSITIVE SIGNS TODAY

All of which prepares us to consider the future of the church's world mission in the seventies. Despite the gloom that has widely settled on older segments of the Protestant church in the West, evangelicals are filled with gratitude to God for what they discern as positive signs of the vitality of God's people throughout the world. First, they find deep significance in the new mood of evangelism currently coming upon the worldwide Protestant church, traceable largely to the inspiration and leadership of three men. R. Kenneth Strachan of the Latin America Mission launched the Evangelism-in-Depth movement in Nicaragua (1960). Although EID began in a small country in Central America, it has produced among churches in many nations

---

[2] *A History of the Expansion of Christianity*, I (New York, 1944), 3.
[3] *A History of Christianity* (New York, 1954), p. 333. I am indebted to Dr. Ralph D. Winter for bringing the Peregrini to my attention.

a new determination to mobilize and train all Christians for the work of continuous and effective evangelism. Spin-off movements have refined its methodology. At present some twenty countries in Africa are involved in intensive and extensive campaigns, variously called New Life For All and Christ For All. Major churches in at least fifteen countries in Asia are being drawn into this pattern of evangelism. 1971 will mark an indigenous Evangelism: Deep and Wide campaign throughout South Vietnam.

When Billy Graham convened the World Congress of Evangelism (Berlin, 1966), he sparked an increasing succession of regional congresses in various parts of the world, some confined to single nations or even separate language groups.

When Donald A. McGavran organized the Institute of Church Growth (Eugene, Oregon, 1960; moved to Fuller Seminary in 1965), he provided an entirely new type of missiological training that harnessed theology and the social sciences with intensive research into the history of the expansion of Christianity and the dynamics of church growth. Evangelicals leaped at the opportunity to study under his direction. During the past decade over 300 experienced Western missionaries and national church leaders have entered this program. They have already produced over eighty book-length research studies. Not a few have been published. From this has come the Church Growth Workshop, a four-day study program held annually for furloughing missionaries and national pastors in various parts of America and in centers overseas. Attendance and interest keep growing. The *Church Growth Bulletin,* particularly designed for career missionaries, is now in its seventh year, and subscriptions exceed 4,000. As a result of all this ferment there is hardly an evangelical graduate seminary in America today that is not upgrading its missions department. All in all, missionaries have never been so carefully selected by their organizations and so thoroughly trained for the cross-cultural communication of the Christian faith, as in our day.

And what has been the result of this renewal of the evangelistic dimension of the church? Despite the secularization of theology in the West, the "new morality" popularized under the rubric of "situation ethics," and the initial popular response given the "Death of God" theology and its "secular city," the decade 1960-1970 saw Christianity spread in an unprecedented fashion through the world. Massive harvests appear to be on the way. David Barrett's studies of the rate of growth of the church in Africa over several decades show that "the entire Christian community has expanded uniformly at a rate over twice that of the population increase."

This leads him to anticipate 350 million African Christians by the turn of the century. "This staggering possibility calls first for dedicated planning of the highest order," and then asks, "Are your missions big enough?" The same question must be asked in the face of the prospect of 50 million Christians in Brazil by A.D. 2000. Indeed, the more the data on church growth throughout the world is gathered and scientifically analyzed, the more concerned evangelicals become about the future. Are they training enough personnel to gather in the harvest that God is manifestly preparing for his church in the days ahead?

This leads us to a second positive sign — the present evolution of missionary societies and the changing roles of their missionaries. Never has there been more serious discussion between mission administrators and national church leaders to achieve greater "partnership in obedience." Even so, the way has not been easy. Stephen Neill has courageously defined the underlying issue:

> ... younger Church leaders sometimes give the impression that they would rather that their fellow-countrymen died as heathen than that they should be brought to the knowledge of Christ by Christians from the West. If such a situation is reached, there is nothing for it but for the older Churches to rebel. A dictatorship of the younger Churches is no better than a dictatorship of the missionary societies. "Partnership" is not a human alliance for mutual convenience, it is PARTNERSHIP IN OBEDIENCE to the command of Christ to preach the Gospel to every creature. If this obedience is lacking on the one side or the other, the partnership would seem to lack a valid foundation. The world situation is changing so rapidly that opportunities are being lost every day. If an older Church seems to hear a clear call to evangelize, it may be necessary that it should go forward, leaving the younger Church to

follow when it is sufficiently awake itself to hear the call.[4]

For instance, what to do in Latin America, at a time when congregations are increasing at the rate of 5,000 a year and training schools are producing future pastors at no more than 600 a year? Some theoreticians have argued that missions should heed the cry, "Go Home!" Actually, the creative response of church and mission has been "Theological Education by Extension," a dynamic operation that has already increased ten-fold in Latin America alone the number of men being trained for pastoral service. Such a program is bringing nationals and foreigners together as never before. The "Macedonian" cry has never been so insistent in calling for more men of training and ability from the West to heighten the effectiveness and scope of this program.

One could list other ways in which missions are changing with the times to provide their missionaries with new roles by which to discharge the mandate to reach the two billion that have yet to hear of Jesus Christ. Bible translation, literacy programs, literature preparation, student evangelism, discipleship training workshops, church growth analyses (how to remove the obstructions standing in the way of the "static church"), visual aids, mass media, lay training programs, etc. The range of cooperative activities is legion. Missionaries are especially grateful for Evangelical Missions Information Service, the common infrastructure of the two major evangelical inter-mission associations (EFMA-IFMA). EMIS pours an unending flow of ideas to church and mission leaders all over the world.

Missions are assisting in the operation of more than fifty "Christian" radio stations which literally cover the whole world with their high wattage signals. Evangelicals are extensively involved in the 800 translation projects currently listed by the United Bible Societies; some are even serving with Roman Catholics in joint projects. By February 1971, Wycliffe Bible Translators had entered 512 tribes and were being approached by two new countries, calling for their services in language reduction, literacy campaigns, and Bible translation. As far as their leadership is concerned, this is not the time for either retrenchment or withdrawal. Never have so many millions enrolled in such a variety of Bible correspondence courses. Some

---

[4] *The Unfinished Task* (London, 1957), p. 165.

missions are finding this tool increasingly effective in reaching Muslims throughout North Africa, the Middle East, and South Asia. The Pentecostal movement has become the "third force" in the Christian church. One section, the Assemblies of God, conducts a worldwide correspondence training program in more than eighty countries. Several hundred thousand potential leaders are being trained. And all the while, God by his Spirit is converting students in the West and speaking to them of their responsibility to put heart, will, and resources to the task of evangelizing their generation, in fellowship with the worldwide "household of faith."

All in all, evangelicals are encouraged as they look abroad in this great day of the worldwide expansion of Christianity. What is particularly heartening is the recent proliferation of mission structures, chiefly lay inspired and lay supported. Some center on home missions, others conduct their operations overseas. Nationals in such disparate nations as Nigeria and Japan, Korea and the Philippines, have involved themselves in this work. In India alone more than a hundred such indigenous groups are engaged in proclaiming the gospel among other Indian peoples who previously had no opportunity to learn of Christ and be incorporated into his church, and some of these societies are eager to send men overseas — to the Middle East, Africa and Southeast Asia.

At this point, however, we should examine the darker side of the picture and detail those problems which give evangelicals considerable reason to pause as they survey the world scene. Obviously, they are not unaware of the great political imponderables of these days. No nation is secure. Overnight, massive civil dislocations could upset the delicate balance of internal and international relationships. But my concern here is with even more tangible problems. By describing them and detailing evangelical response, I hope to cast yet more light on the future of missions in the seventies.

PROTESTANT CHURCH STRUCTURES

Evangelical ambivalence is never so apparent as when the Ecumenical Movement (WCC) is under consideration. On the one hand, evangelicals refuse to measure the success of the Christian world mission by the increase in denominational mergers, regional council activities or the expansion of inter-church aid. While the importance of some of these things may be recognized, none are regarded as crucial to mission, as biblically understood. On one point all evangelicals are agreed. They refuse to define mission in terms that mute or omit the indispensability and finality of Jesus Christ. "There is no other name under heaven given among men by which we must be saved" (Acts 4:12).

Over the years, evangelicals have seen a steady erosion of missionary concern within the conciliar movement. Prior to 1961, it was widely heralded that the merger of the church (WCC) and mission (IMC) streams that flowed from the 1910 World Missionary Conference in Edinburgh (where the modern Ecumenical Movement was born) would realize the lofty dream that gripped the Archbishop of Canterbury at that time: "It is my single thought tonight — that the place of missions in the life of the Church must be the central place, and no other."[5] At the Fourth Assembly of the WCC (1968), however, its leadership candidly spoke of "widespread defeatism in the churches about the work of evangelism and world mission" (Niles). Indeed, by that time mission as traditionally understood had been largely eclipsed, if not altogether replaced, by a reconception of the gospel foreign to the New Testament.[6]

Evangelicals are sufficiently acquainted with the expansion of Christianity, the growth of churches, and the origins of missionary societies to realize that the world would never have been evangelized to the extent that it has if the task of mission had been borne solely by church administrators. Nonconformists such as Xavier and Wesley, Carey and Judson, and thousands of others, both men and women, came under the constraint of the love of Christ and took the gospel to the heathen, often without the encouragement or backing of the religious establishment, whether Protestant or Roman.

Not a few evangelicals belong to WCC member churches. As such, they are not unwilling to participate in their outreach in mission. As there is no Protestant church without its evangelicals, so there is no mission agency, conciliar or otherwise, in which

[5] William Richey Hogg, *Ecumenical Foundations* (New York, 1952), p. 123.

[6] Arthur F. Glasser, "What Has Been the Evangelical Stance, New Delhi to Uppsala?" *Evangelical Missions Quarterly*, V, 3 (Spring 1969), 129-150.

they cannot be found. And yet, at least three-fourths of all American missionaries come from nonconciliar churches and serve in missions outside the WCC framework.[7] This does not mean that these missions all assume the same posture toward the WCC. Some are willing to cooperate with national churches "of like faith and obedience" irrespective of ecclesiastical relationships. One of the oldest (1865) so-called "Faith" missions (IFMA), the China Inland Mission of Hudson Taylor fame (now the Overseas Missionary Fellowship), is presently collaborating with the Anglican Church in Malaysia and most major churches in Indonesia, even to the extent of sending workers to them. Increasingly, evangelicals are displaying a willingness to receive and work with all whom Christ has manifestly received. The extent of this cooperation, however, rarely extends above the level of the local congregation. This is largely due to "profound distrust of the Ecumenical Movement" (Smith) and the determination to avoid even the semblance of indifference to or coresponsibility for its doctrinal defection from or reinterpretation of the biblical norm.

THE ROMAN CATHOLIC CHURCH

Evangelicals have long sought to share Jesus Christ and the gospel with Roman Catholics, at home and overseas. In the past, their attitudes toward the Roman Catholic Church have been largely conditioned by the Reformation, and the sharp lines of doctrinal difference defined by the Reformers. Today, however, they are more aware of the political and sociological dimensions of that sixteenth-century struggle. Furthermore, they do not see the doctrinal polarities in the same sharp light. Looking back,

---

[7] For details, consult Ralph D. Winter, "The New Missions and the Mission of the Church," *International Review of Mission*, LX, 237, 89-100; also his reference to Donald F. Durnbaugh, *The Believer's Church* (New York, 1968), p. 238. The statistics: Division of Overseas Ministries (DOM-NCCCUSA)—32 organizations and 8279 missionaries; Interdenominational Foreign Mission Association (IFMA)—44 organizations and 5976 missionaries; Evangelical Foreign Missions Association (EFMA)—63 organizations and 6611 missionaries; Fellowship of Missions (FOM)—5 organizations and 841 missionaries; The Associated Missions (TAM-ICCC)—9 organizations and 185 missionaries; Non-Affiliated—426 organizations and 10,980 missionaries (North American Protestant Ministries Overseas [Monrovia, Cal., MARC, 1970], pp. 162-172, 9th edition).

they can see bigotry and imperfect understanding of Scripture on both sides. In these days of universal education and freedom of inquiry, evangelical Protestants are beginning to encounter evangelical Catholics. But they have long hoped that the Roman Catholic Church might understand and proclaim "the way of God more perfectly," and have prayed to this end. As a result, they could not but be increasingly drawn to Pope John XXIII in his efforts to bring *aggiornamento* to the church, especially when he called for a Vatican Council to redefine the nature and function of the church in spiritual rather than juridical terms. "He was the best Pope Protestants ever had." Many of the changes brought about by Vatican II are "wholesome, the work of the Holy Spirit, and a source of joy to evangelicals" (Henry). They have learned the folly of the sterile contention that nothing can change in the Roman Catholic Church. As a result, a new openness has characterized their approach to Catholics and their literature. Sometimes Hans Küng sounds like an evangelical; Rahner's obscure categories remind them of Tillich; the text of "Gospel and Revolution," drafted by sixteen bishops of the Third World, is more acceptable to evangelical missiologists than any WCC document on the same theme.[8] The most "Protestant" Catholic document I know is the *Decree on the Church's Missionary Activity (Ad Gentes)*, Vatican II. And yet, in the face of their growing awareness of Rome's spectrum of theological opinion, ranging from conservative to radical, evangelicals draw back. How does its inclusivism differ from conciliar Protestantism?

On the other hand, evangelicals are now aware as never before that many loyal Catholics know and love Jesus Christ with an intimacy and devotion surpassing their own. They cannot but be grateful to God for the widespread interest of Catholics in the Bible and in religious conversation.[9] They are becoming increasingly aware of a groundswell of spiritual hunger among many whose previous interest seemed formal and minimal. Billy Graham has a large following among them. Other evangelical radio programs are followed with close attention. Most

---

[8] For this text see *New Theology No. 6*, ed. Martin E. Marty and Dean G. Peerman (New York, 1969), pp. 243-254.

[9] A surprising number of Catholics are among the million and a half members of Scripture Union, an evangelical Bible-reading fellowship whose materials are published in more than 150 languages.

participants in Inter-Varsity Christian Fellowship or Campus Crusade for Christ have visited Catholic campus activities, in America and overseas.

It is anyone's guess what the ultimate outcome will be of this casual disregard of ecclesiastical relationships. There is every possibility that inter-communion exchange, with its experiential sharing of Christ in Bible study, corporate prayer, and testimonial fellowship, could generate a new worldwide movement that will greatly forward the mission of the church, touching the "two billion."[10] One thing is unmistakably clear: Protestant evangelicals are much closer, in theology and commitment, to many Catholics than to the heterodox liberals within Protestantism. And they unabashedly identify these new stirrings and alignments as evidence of God's continuing grace to man. He will build his church and the powers of death shall not prevail against it (Matt. 16:18).

SOCIAL SERVICE AND SOCIAL ACTION

Evangelicals bristle when charged with ignoring "the whole man" in their preoccupation with his soul. They read history differently. The Reformation churches mounted no crusade to abolish slavery. This was accomplished by the converts and free-church movements rooted in the Evangelical Awakening. It was they who descended into the slums and sought to grapple with the social evils created by the Industrial Revolution. They called for sobriety and discipline in personal and family life. Down through the years, the budgets of their missions have always contained massive allocations for educational and medical service.

Evangelicals, however, have always resisted the temptation to confine the church's mission to man-in-society, the cultural mandate. No! Man must be reconciled to God! The evangelistic mandate Christ gave his church must be carried out! It is true that in earlier decades of this century, evangelicals overreacted against the "Social Gospel" movement. They gave the appearance of being almost hostile to the massive stream of cultural obligation that courses throughout Scripture. Today, in the

---

10 "... the Gospel message has not yet been heard, or scarcely so, by two billion human beings" ("Lumen Gentium," *The Documents of Vatican II* (New York, 1966), p. 597.

seventies, evangelicals are charged with all the selfish aberrations of the political right. Unfortunately, reactionary elements have long existed in their midst and have lacked breadth of concern for man in the totality of his need. But evangelicalism's more moderate leaders are painfully conscious of their failure to speak prophetically on such issues as racism, economic exploitation, political corruption, and American insularity. They are sadly aware of occasions in the past when the most perceptive evangelicals uncritically reflected the ignorance and prejudices of their generation. Actually, recent research into the social involvement of the churches in America demonstrates that all are guilty in one way or another. Even the Social Gospel movement at its height was almost completely silent about "white racism" — the most grievous social issue facing America in the seventies.

Looking ahead, it seems likely that evangelicals will continue to be ambivalent about the call to social action. Too much is at stake. They particularly react against the line currently popular in conciliar circles, that the church should be willing to resort to violence to remedy social evils. They know that whenever this was done in the past it did not bring undiluted relief. The long history of the church too easily substantiates the thesis of Jacques Ellul: Whenever Christians poured their strength into defending the poor, and resorted to violence to achieve what they regarded as good ends, this crowded out all the rest of their Christianity and ended in "total abandonment of faith, in indifference to revelation, and in the atheism that appears to be the normal revolutional position."[11] Evangelicals regard "theologies of revolution" as virtually devoid of concern for man's spiritual plight, in his alienation from God. They are almost persuaded that Ellul is right when he concludes, "Today's theologians of violence are pharisees, terrible distorters of Christian truth" (p. 140).

So then, evangelicals are adamant in their rejection of the current semantic and exegetical confusion that equates evangelism with politics. Of course, they will continue to "remember the poor," as the Apostle Paul admonished (Gal. 2:10). They will continue to proclaim the gospel "by word and deed" (Rom.

---

[11] *Violence: Reflections from a Christian Perspective* (New York, 1969), p. 22.

15:10), performing works of mercy and assistance, while "beseeching men on behalf of Christ to be reconciled to God" (II Cor. 5:20).

But this does not mean they will ignore their political responsibilities. There is a growing desire among men to be more positive in rendering to Caesar the things that are Caesar's, while jealously guarding their primary obligation to render to God the things that are God's (Matt. 22:21). A case in point: Pentecostals are often accused of being totally indifferent to Caesar. But is this actually the case? Go to Brazil and observe what they are doing at the ballot box and through their elected representatives to establish justice in society. Actually, a prominent American Methodist bishop did just that. What he saw touched him deeply. He felt pressed to write a letter to the editor of *The Christian Century* to share the good news. He concluded, "It seems to me ... [they] have much to teach the churches of both Latin and North America."[12]

CONCLUSION

What of the future? Evangelicals are not unmoved by today's shifting tides of thought and inquiry, nor are they blind to the rise and fall of church and mission structures. True, they are sobered by the increasing tempo discerned in the cosmic conflict between God and Satan in the human arena. But they resist the temptation to despair. They are deeply persuaded that "all

---

[12] James Armstrong, Bishop of the United Methodist Church, Dakotas Area, in a letter to the editor of *The Christian Century*, February 17, 1971, p. 228. Incidentally, in this same issue there is an extended analysis of Urbana '70. The author, William R. Wineke, states: "The conference would have been an eye-opener to any liberal churchman who looks upon evangelicals as narrow, closed-mind types who want to live in the past century. For one thing, it proclaimed a de facto ecumenism that would shock even the leaders of the Consultation on Church Union." Mr. Wineke was particularly impressed with the combination of evangelistic zeal and passion for social justice he witnessed at this gathering, and concluded: "This emphasis on the need for salvation, and on the centrality of the Bible for any kind of Christian activity, is a bond that the evangelicals share, no matter what other differences they may have. Without that bond, the tensions between young and old would almost surely prove divisive. With it, they might just learn to live together. And if they do that, they will have a lot to teach the rest of us" ("Evangelical Students at Urbana '70: Zeal and Social Passion," pp. 226-27).

human history shall be consummated in Christ" (Eph. 1:10, Phillips). This presses them to hold fast their Lord's mandate that "the gospel must first be published among all nations" (Mark 13:10). This must remain the central priority.

Were you to ask the average evangelical missionary how he regards the future he might recall Adoniram Judson's reply to a similar question, put to him in Burma more than a hundred years ago. At the time all manner of adversaries had crowded in and were mockingly challenging his faith. His reply was a timeless evangelical affirmation. In his own quiet way, he said: "The outlook, Sir, is as bright as the promises of God." And so it was. As then, so now.

F. DEAN LUEKING has been in the parish ministry at Grace Lutheran Church, River Forest, Illinois since 1954, serving as pastor since 1962. As a part of his study at Concordia Seminary, St. Louis, he worked in Japan from 1951 to 1953 as a vicar in Japanese Lutheran congregations in and around Yokohama. Following his ordination in 1954, he continued graduate studies at the University of Chicago, where he received his doctorate in church history in 1960. His dissertation was published under the title *Mission in the Making*. His other books include *A Century of Caring* and *While It Is Day*. He has co-authored a study in ecumenics entitled *Grace Under Pressure*. Along with his pastoral duties he serves on the board of directors of the *Christian Century* magazine, the *Academy of Parish Clergy*, and the Wheat Ridge Foundation, and is associate editor of *Lutheran Forum*.

8

F. Dean Lueking: The Local Church

THE ONE THING CERTAIN ABOUT THE FUTURE OF THE CHRISTIAN world mission is that it will be involved with people. It is now involved with people. It has always been involved with people. God shall meet people with the good news of his redeeming love in Jesus Christ, even as he has done in the past and is doing now.

I want to briefly describe a number of people who have come to me in my work as a local parish pastor. Although these people are individuals, they are also types. Each represents a certain kind of person, and each represents certain challenges, that will confront the mission of the local congregation in the future.

I. MEETING THOSE IN SEARCH OF AN INNER LIFE

His red hair reaches his shoulders, not at all unkempt but nonetheless an unmistakable reminder of his present identity with the growing subculture of rock music, cultural change, hallucinogenic drugs, and a bagful of vague ideas about freedom, peace, and the cosmos. He is just past his nineteenth birthday. He is a college freshman on a campus that advertises its 20,000 students as a sign that education must surely be going on there. He is remarkably cheerful in spite of the muddle of trying to learn something in classes of 800, the instructor seen and heard by closed-circuit TV. Last year, as a high school senior in a midwestern suburban community, he was among the 40 per cent of his class who smoked grass (a classmate from California put the percentage at 90). He was also among the

30 per cent in his class who went on to LSD. Between February and August of 1969 he experienced forty-five LSD trips. His parents knew nothing of the situation until mid-summer. And shortly after he revealed his deep involvement in mind-expanding drugs, he stopped using them. The terror of the onset of a trip without LSD, coupled with remorse, nearly constant headaches, and the acceptance and love of an above-average family circle combined to make him stop.

He speaks of all this in less than an hour in my study and caps the conversation by asking what the Christian gospel and community of faith could mean for him. He had been exposed to the essentials of the Way as a youth in Sunday School and confirmation classes. But the traditionally programmed, one-doctrine-and-another form of presentation had offered him little in the way of genuine inner spirituality. He is not bitter about his Christian past, but that past is remote. What truly took me by surprise was his somewhat shy question about whether there were still thirty minutes left for meditation. Wanting to show me what he does each day, he opened his guitar case, set upon my desk an eight by ten picture of an Indian mystic, and took out a paperback on the discipline of the inner life. Then he proceeded to put me out of his mind and concentrate on guitar chords, incantations, and the gentle compulsion of those eyes peering at him from the photograph.

This troubled, promising young man is part of a very considerable body of people in the Western world who are groping for an inner spiritual illumination and are turning to Eastern mysticism — often via rock music — to satisfy that longing. It is not altogether to the point that such a youth may drive to class in a Porsche and devour NFL games all Sunday afternoon. Nor is it to the point that a yoga instructor has to tell his suburban matron class that they will hardly experience satori by trying to splice a harried half hour of spiritual discipline into an afternoon schedule of chauffering the children to Cub Scouts and dancing class without being late for husband at the commuter train. The point is that millions of Westerners are seeking an antidote to the programmed, computerized, mechanized consumer-culture we live in, which has much to say to man the producer and man the operator but little or nothing to say to man the spiritual being.

Christians, then, may well inquire into that aspect of the church's spiritual heritage which puts a premium upon the genuineness of inner spiritual experience. Looking toward the future of the Christian world mission, with an eye on the nineteen-year-old redhead with a guitar and a paperback on yoga, pastors and parishioners should recognize that they are going to find the great Christian mystics of the past increasingly useful, as well as those men of spirituality in the present. People are becoming progressively bored, if not dismayed, with the longer segments of leisure, the decreasing personal contacts, the greater mobility, and the increasing affluence contemporary life has brought. They are learning that the relentless pounding of gadget-oriented media finally wearies the inner spirit: things do not go better with Coke nor do the friendly skies belong to United. The Christian community will find that an increasing number of young adults will not be impressed whatsoever by the institutions, thought processes, activist accomplishments of a thousand years of Western Christendom. But they will stop and take a second look at those who exhibit an interest in the depths of the Johannine writings of the New Testament, or in the inner wholeness of that sophisticated modern man of international affairs who traced the landscape of his soul in *Markings*. Western Christians can welcome an increased exchange with Eastern Christianity. We have something to learn from those who have not been afraid of silence, of contemplation, of Tradition, of the Holy Spirit acting upon the human spirit, the Christ-in-us as well as the Christ-for-us. True, we have some adapting, not wholesale adopting to undertake. After all, our ancestors have not eaten rice for a thousand years. The temptation to wallow in the bizarre and the superficial will be constant. The danger of confusing any kind of interior glow with the gospel of cosmic reconciliation and redemption in Jesus Christ will be potent. But clues are at hand. I have already alluded to Dag Hammarskjöld. John XXIII had a hearing and will continue to have a place in the Christian witness not only because of Vatican II but especially because of a hearty and healthy spirituality that moved him outward to men of other faiths and to men of no faith. Significantly, he expressed it under the title *Journey of a Soul*. The gentle, disciplined men of the Taizé Community have already established helpful links with

Christians in the ghetto of Chicago. John Ylvisaker is a portent of the type of liturgist who will reach the campus generation. Martin Luther King, Jr., was a rare blend of inner spiritual integrity with activism; his legacy will continue to be powerful and his creative adaptation of Gandhian techniques instructive. Perhaps the more important matter at the moment is not the extent to which these Christians speak directly to non-Christians, but the measure in which such people help pastors and parishioners to recover a neglected aspect of the whole Christian heritage, the interior life that is created and guided by the Spirit in such a way as to keep people attentive and appreciative of the things that, though unseen, are eternal (II Cor. 4:18).

II. BEARING WITH THE DISAFFECTED

"I don't come to church to hear you preach politics: I just want to hear the gospel." This is her way of putting me and several hundred thousand other clergy of the land into a corner we don't belong in at all. She is outraged at the suggestion of taking the Kerner Report seriously or even listening to its diagnosis of what threatens the continuance of our society. She has the universe neatly divided into two camps, liberal and conservative — with little doubt about which side the angels are on. She wants the whole content of divine revelation sorted out and nailed down in unchanging categories of doctrine, supported by an inerrant Bible, dominated by the Law, insensitive to the possibilities of the transcendent and mysterious, and enshrined in rigidly conformist traditions of worship and polity. She resents the implication that the Parable of the Good Samaritan and the Twenty-fifth Chapter of St. Matthew have contemporary meaning. The poor, by and large, deserve their lot because of their laziness. The chief enemy of the church in America is not Mammon, but Marx. Thus the World Council of Churches is an abomination, since it includes within its ranks Christians from the Communist lands. She is offended by the idea that she is a racial bigot; she simply affirms that God has clearly assigned the black man his place.

She was relatively happy in the congregation through the 1950's. As long as the sermon took us all back to an idealized first century and left us there, the congregation had nothing to complain about. But then came the successive shock waves of the 1960's: Kennedy's murder in Dallas, the riots in Watts and Detroit, the escalation of the war in Vietnam, Black Power, campus revolt, the anti-war movement, and the increasingly shrill rhetoric of crisis, revolution, hunger, and exploding population.

Through all of this she yearned to hear from the pulpit the reassurance that God's will — that is, laissez-faire political theory, the capitalist system, the Republican Party, and the editorial opinion of the *Chicago Tribune* — will ultimately be done. But she has not heard this. Words strange and new to her ear — "prophetic," "renewal," "reconciliation," "relevance," "servanthood" — have left her disillusioned. These are not the old, familiar words. Everything used to be so clear-cut, with most of the church-talk beginning with "You ought" or "You must." But now it has changed into the slippery "Let us therefore celebrate," and a bewildering reference to "man come of age" under the "God of the secular." Her thought world is formed by *Human Events, U. S. News and World Report,* and the political speeches of George Wallace. Her suspicions about the denomination in general and the congregation and pastor in particular are backed by yellow journalism circulating within and sometimes beyond the denomination.

There are reasons for her disaffection.

The first is that she is reflecting a certain strand of her own spiritual training. She was taught a semi-heretical form of Christian belief, highly individualistic, law-oriented, other-worldly, and virtually without any sense of the horizontal dimension of the reconciling power of the gospel. That demon of her past has suddenly erupted, to the detriment of her soul and the dismay of her pastor. The pastor, in fact, has a greater responsibility for her plight than she does.

Second, she has not been willing to recognize her own idolatry. For this she bears direct responsibility. Repentance has always meant someone else to her. She has contrived an ersatz religion of social acceptability, philanthropy, and the patronage of popular, kept preachers who thrive by forever baptizing the status quo. She has willfully put herself outside the message of the gospel and cannot hear it as the self-offering of God

119

himself for her smug, defensive, unhappy existence that has turned in upon itself with disastrous results.

Third, she has been wronged by clergy who insist on being at the eye of every storm, who will travel the length of the land under the pretext of being "prophetic," but who have not the time, the love, or the intestinal fortitude to ring the local doorbell and sit down with those who share her dilemma. Such men suffer, not from what the Apostle Paul called the "daily anxiety over the churches," but from an acute fear of being left out of news reports or the petty limelight of denominational glory.

And so her heart is hardened. And she has taken it out on the church in the only manner she knows how: personal and economic boycott. Her net worth runs beyond six figures. Last year she gave $20 toward the work of the congregation. This year she gave nothing. But no one seems to care. No one stands by with a Power to exorcise the demon that has possessed her. Where are those who will outlast her disaffection by constancy in prayer and who will outlast her cantankerousness by a Love that bears and believes and endures all things?

The woman I am describing is part of an increasing, not a diminishing, number. Jeffrey Haddon's recent book *The Gathering Storm in the Churches* predicts, in fact, that the widening gap between clergy and laity will cut through all denominational lines in the coming decades. Haddon sees a growing cleavage among Christians on the question of how the church relates to social problems in the world, a cleavage that could render the traditional alignments according to doctrine and polity obsolete and bring about new groupings of Christians on the basis of social action or reaction. There is already ample evidence to make such a thesis plausible.

However, the past five years of ministry and mission in the local congregation make me unwilling to accept such a situation as Haddon predicts, and I am confident that I am not speaking only for myself or for the congregation I serve. I prefer another image, that of *the church in mission to herself*. That sounds like a contradiction in terms. But this phrase, taken from a recent statement on the Christian mission,[1] does speak to realities and

---

[1] In 1965 the Lutheran Church-Missouri Synod adopted six affirmations on God's mission which speak impressively of the church's calling to the

opens up alternatives to polarization when applied by the local congregation to its own disaffected segment. I know by experience what so many others know, that drop-out Christians must be a target for the Christian mission. The future before us cannot be envisioned without taking into account this segment of Western Christendom that has broken off from the community of the forgiven and gone its own, unhappy way. Such ministry is exceedingly hard work, is very time-consuming, and is always one-to-one. It is comparable to the Christian presence in Muslim lands. Our brothers there have learned what it means to sow the seed and wait, and to rejoice over the *one* sheep that is returned to the fold.

In recent years of ministry to disaffected Christians I have learned the limits of the Sunday-morning sermon from the pulpit as a way of communication. Not that preaching has no function at all in conveying the social implications of the gospel. By no means. But genuine lay engagement in explosive human problems inevitably calls for a setting in which two-way conversation can occur. Clarification, deepening biblical awareness, and the sharpening of focus on specific problems in the human context of the day call for give and take between pastor and people. Small groups, open forums, and random conversation are useful means to exchange experiences and to encourage those attitudes disaffected Christians need. Some pastors stand in the pulpit, hand down ultimatums on race, war, hunger, and the generation gap, but never stop to listen, learn, suffer, and grow with their people. Those parishioners who disagree or who are troubled can only react in resentment, without so much as a chance to inquire for a more adequate understanding of the directives of the Faith in the modern world. I am unimpressed

---

whole world, the whole society, the whole man. The third affirmation is entitled: "The Church is Christ's Mission to the Church" and reads in part:

> In obedience to the church's Head and in sanctified loyalty to his congregation and his church body, a Christian will be ready with good conscience both to witness and to listen to all Christians. . . . Because the church is Christ's mission to the church, Christians should speak the Word of God to one another as they nurture, edify, and educate one another for Christian faith and life.

Like all good ecclesiastical pronouncements, these splendid statements have yet to be truly absorbed into the congregations of the Synod. They represent a goal to be reached rather than a description of the present status.

by the wailings and hand-wringing of clergy who conclude that the parish is dead because there has not been total and immediate response to pulpit pronouncements. There is a better way.

I have seen suburban and inner-city Christians come together in cell groups over a period of several years, listening and learning together, disagreeing basically without breaking off from each other, and discovering new levels of unity without denying their distinctiveness as persons. This dialogue is in itself a notable, miraculous thing! But more to the point is the influence such Christians exercise on those others in the congregation who take a dim view of nearly anything that requires the discomfort of thinking a new thought and experiencing some of the consequences of living in the world as the people of God. The congregation has not split down the middle, as some dire predictions warned several years ago, and it need not split in the future. People have grown by listening and talking to each other. Certainly, we have not fulfilled our mission calling. But the gospel continues to be that power among us that forgives, reconciles, and motivates. We get cranky and upset, but the love of Christ constrains us, and we are learning how to outlast each other's frustrations in the spirit of forbearance. There will be much room for this as congregations must continue to participate in the Christian mission to the disaffected, who can so easily drift into oblivion or into the heresies of the Radical Right.

III. INNOVATORS IN MISSION IN THE BLACK GHETTO

A third person typifying the tasks that will continue to confront the local congregation in mission is seventeen, black, and a resident in a public-housing high-rise apartment which puts one thousand human beings under a single roof. Thirty-two of these vast, concrete warrens cover a strip of ground in the inner city two miles long and one-third of a mile wide. Some 35,000 people are jammed together in living conditions the city fathers love to boast about as urban renewal. Seasoned political minds say that the original idea was to keep a dependable block of Democratic votes handy in these apartment structures. The political organization is deeply entrenched from city hall downward. But something has backfired tragically. Less than 8 per cent of the residents are working fathers. Eighty-five per cent of the residents are under voting age. In the matriarchal society which prevails, most of the adults are exhausted mothers trying to keep a family of five or ten together, and many cannot read or write.

This is the context in which this lad in his upper teens lives. He is a high school dropout. The last classroom he sat in had only thirty desks for a class of fifty students. He tired of constantly arriving to find no place to sit, and he quit school a few weeks after his sophomore year began. He is too young for the draft, and too young also to have many employers take him seriously for a job. He is unsure of what training opportunities for any kind of life work await him.

At this moment the main influence upon his life comes from the gang to which he belongs. This is the one place that gives him a sense of identity, that accepts him for what he is as a person, and that promises some ideas on what he might do with his life. At the head of this gang is a twenty-three-year-old black resident who lives with his wife and children in the same high rise. Each Tuesday evening this gang leader meets with approximately forty other gang leaders in the basement of the nearby Roman Catholic Church. The strategy sessions range over a wide area of problems the gang members face: bail money, medical care, inter-gang rumbles, jobs, keeping a number of very tentative, legitimate businesses going (a restaurant and grocery outlet), and the overriding issue that is constantly before them — police harassment. The Gang Intelligence Unit of the local city police force operates on the principle that all gangs are bad and that the only proper tactic is to break them up and prevent them from forming any political or economic leverage. That is why the leader was arrested on an alleged assault and battery charge a year ago, held for $75,000 bail, and released from the county jail after two months detention. Reason for dismissal: lack of evidence.

The seventeen-year-old knows and trusts his gang leader. That is the chief reason he has not put in his bid to join the Black Panthers, who are serving breakfasts for children in the church building nearest his apartment, and are instructing them in the coming revolution. He is impressed by the Panthers. "At

123

least they're doing something for hungry kids." But he is not too sure he can accept the stringent requirements the Panthers lay down for members, and that is why he hasn't bothered to get the full story on what one must do to qualify and stay in the Panther organization.

Slightly more than two miles away, a black pastor carries on an overburdened ministry in another section of the ghetto. He knows the seventeen-year-old. The two met at the church building where the Panthers moved in for their breakfast program. The previous pastor, a young white clergyman who came to the ghetto straight from the seminary six years ago, found the Panther issue his final undoing. He was willing to let the Panthers in, and to depend upon the black members of the congregation to work out the problems (they were by no means of one mind on the matter). But denominational officials downtown sent a directive explaining that the Panthers had to go immediately. The young pastor asked them to come in person and enact the directive. They demurred, suggesting that the neighboring black pastor be their spokesman. He refused. The white pastor then left for a new charge in another city. Now the black pastor has been asked to minister to the orphaned congregation. He cannot possibly find the time and energy to do so. The seventeen-year-old black youth is quite well informed about all these developments and is intrigued by the possibilities of what may eventually happen.

Several months ago he received a surprise. One of the black parishioners, a resident of the same high rise, left his job at the post office and let the word get around that he was entering something new, called the Black Diaconate. The neighboring black pastor had accepted the responsibility for training and guiding six laymen already chosen for the group. Their responsibilities looked strikingly similar to those of the gang leader. They were to go to hospitals, businesses, schools, and the courts — wherever people were in the daily rounds of life with its problems — and try to help. In addition, they were to conduct worship services in the church building and in the apartment units of members, they were to teach both youths and adults basic Christianity, they were to counsel and to coach, and they were to attend instruction classes for themselves.

The Black Diaconate has been the first real sign of life the teenage boy has seen among Christians in the ghetto. He knows all about the storefront churches and holds them in contempt. It is not the storefront that offends him, but the open dishonesty and opportunism of the preachers who come and go regularly. The former white pastor was well intentioned but woefully ill-prepared. But now a number of young men from the community itself have volunteered for service as deacons. The black pastor in charge of their training told them that this was not something new in Christendom; the pattern goes back to the Book of Acts.

The Black Deacons work closely with gang leaders. They have had to constantly explain that the Black Deacons are not just another gang. Having grown up in the neighborhood and knowing the turf from personal experience, they are uniquely equipped to reach the seventeen-year-old. In this respect they have definite advantages over their pastor-bishop, and enormous advantages over those men in the denominational office downtown who handle their salary and living stipend while they are in training. This is to continue for three years, after which they are to be offered to the church for placement wherever they can best serve.

The number of youths now living in urban ghettos in North and South America and sharing the basic problems of survival with this lad runs into the millions. Their situation is very different from that of the first youth described in this essay. That young man's needs are not needs for survival. His high- or middle-class environment offers him every convenience. For the young man of the ghetto, however, the problems are food on the table, some kind of work to do, a sense of identity, and how to stay out of jail. The future of the Christian world mission cannot exist apart from a creative, effective outreach toward this youth and the many he represents.

The Black Diaconate is a tiny but instructive clue to how the mission may be mobilized in the heart of our great urban centers. People are set aside who know what it is to struggle and live in the ghetto. Their training is on the spot. Their relationships to people in and beyond the Christian community are direct. The cost of such ventures is minimal in relation to the potential they represent. In the long run, they will do more for the church at large than vice versa. They are the most creative men in mission and ministry in the United States since the circuit riders rode the frontier a century ago. Inseparable from their own future is a growing consciousness of what Black Theology means. I am not the interpreter of that development, which holds both peril and promise. The peril seems obvious. If what we are talking about is a fundamental departure from the Apostolic Tradition, a theology no longer anchored in the covenant, Calvary, and the open tomb, then something other than Christianity is emerging. But if this development is a faithful, creative appropriation of the Tradition amidst the realities of today's black experience, then the promise is great indeed. The outcome will be given us by black Christians. Our calling is to remain teachable.

IV. AT THE PARISH LINE

A college freshman, a disaffected Christian woman, and a ghetto youth hardly exhaust the kinds of people the local congregation will confront in the future. But the future will certainly include these three — in an endless variety of settings — and they have offered here a means to demonstrate the way we must take our place in local mission, responsive to the gospel and attentive to people as we encounter them where they are.

Robert Pierce Beaver is one of those teachers in the church who has helped us see the larger meaning of the Christian mission as that mission not only works outward but penetrates inward into the life and culture shared by the Christian at home. What Professor Beaver has set forth to us in his quiet, painstakingly thorough manner, is proving to be a heritage of enduring worth at the parish line. We salute him gratefully and thank God for his ministry of teaching. As we enter the future and continue the mission, we will be enriched in all aspects of the church's life by the seasoned perspective of this missionary statesman and walking encyclopedia of mission history. Partnership with him and men of like mind and spirit is no small reason why we look forward with hopeful anticipation to the great things God will do as he brings to fulfillment his purposes in Christ for all men.

GERALD H. ANDERSON, a minister of the United Methodist Church, is the president of Scarritt College for Christian Workers in Nashville, Tennessee. From 1960 to 1970 he was a missionary in the Philippines, serving as Professor of Church History and Ecumenics both at Union Theological Seminary near Manila and in the federated faculty of the Southeast Asia Graduate School of Theology. A former Fulbright Scholar, he studied at the universities of Marburg, Geneva, and Edinburgh, and received his Ph.D. from Boston University. He is the editor and co-author of *The Theology of the Christian Mission, Christ and Crisis in Southeast Asia,* and *Studies in Philippine Church History,* and he is co-editor of *The Concise Dictionary of the Christian World Mission.*

9

Gerald H. Anderson: Mission Research, Writing, and Publishing

Speaking in 1969 to a group of religious book publishers, Martin E. Marty observed that "religious books are in trouble because of the revolution in religion and in the churches." At the end of "the most productive, most exciting, most bewildering, and probably most prosperous decade American religious book publishing has known," he said, "there are good reasons to be concerned about the collapse of the industry." This publishing crisis is particularly true of books dealing with the Christian world mission. Why?

The answer, in brief, was suggested by Norman A. Horner when he wrote recently that "the Protestant missionary enterprise has undergone more radical change in the last fifteen years than in the previous century."[1] A similar situation prevails in the Roman Catholic Church. Many factors, discussed elsewhere in this volume, have contributed to the radical change, but a major manifestation of the new situation is the sharply declining interest of the churches in North America, Great Britain, and Europe for the mission of the church beyond the North Atlantic region. An isolationist mood has settled upon the churches, with concern for mission at home preempting concern for mission around the world. The result is a shrinking market for books dealing with the Christian world mission, and a consequent

[1] *Protestant Crosscurrents in Mission* (Nashville, 1968), p. 10.

reluctance on the part of many publishers to produce books of this nature.

Yet in this critical period there are still signs of hope and vitality. The two most creative and aggressive publishers of world mission studies in the English language are Friendship Press, which is the publishing imprint of the Department of Education for Mission of the National Council of Churches of Christ in the U.S.A., and the William B. Eerdmans Publishing Company in Grand Rapids, Michigan. Friendship Press is

> a cooperative agency through which 26 denominations plan and produce, interdenominationally, annual programs of educational materials concerning the church's mission at home and abroad. It produces annually more than a million pieces.... The purpose is to create an informed constituency on the worldwide mission responsibility of the churches.[2]

Eerdmans, a private Protestant publishing firm, launched its "Christian World Mission Books" in 1968 with R. Pierce Beaver as editor. This bold venture has been projected as "a library of paperback volumes on every aspect of the world mission of the church of Christ — history, theory, methods, functional approaches, regional studies, biography, and also source material."[3] The early volumes in the series are an impressive token of much that is yet to come. Eerdmans also publishes the very useful "Church Growth Books," edited by Donald A. McGavran, which study the problems and patterns of church growth in various countries of Asia, Africa, and Latin America.

Several Protestant denominational publishing houses make significant contributions to world mission literature from time to time, and Maryknoll Publications is the most active among Roman Catholic publishers. In England, Lutterworth Press, which is the publishing house of the United Society for Christian Literature, and the Student Christian Movement Press maintain their commitment to world mission. But world mission

---

[2] William C. Walzer, "National Council of the Churches of Christ in the U.S.A., Department of Education for Mission," *Encyclopedia of Modern Christian Missions*, ed. Burton L. Goddard (Camden, N.J., 1967), p. 462.

[3] R. Pierce Beaver, "Editorial Foreword," *All Loves Excelling: American Protestant Women in World Mission* (Grand Rapids, Mich., 1968), p. 7.

books from the large secular publishing houses, both in North America and in England, are appearing less and less frequently.

One of the most encouraging developments in recent years is the publication of an increasing number of mission studies by the university presses. These academic publishers, committed to advance knowledge even when it is not commercially profitable, have been willing to publish mission studies which meet their high standards of scholarship and come within their scope of specialization. In my own field of work, for instance, three volumes have recently appeared from university presses: *The Jesuits in the Philippines, 1581-1768* by H. de la Costa, S.J. — Harvard; *Nationalism and Christianity in the Philippines* by Richard L. Deats — Southern Methodist University; and *Studies in Philippine Church History*, an ecumenical symposium — Cornell.

Another significant development was the establishment in 1967 of the Missions Advanced Research and Communication Center (MARC) in Monrovia, California. MARC, a division of World Vision International in cooperation with the School of World Mission at Fuller Theological Seminary, is using the latest information systems and computer technology in developing an information center on world Christianity. It is projected that this "World Christian Data Bank," with a microfilm fast retrieval (four-second response) storage system, will eventually contain data on every mission, every missionary, and every church in the world, so that it can produce a continuous and comprehensive picture of the progress of the church in the world. The Center, like its parent organization, is theologically conservative, but attempts to establish information exchange on as broad a basis as possible. MARC cooperates with the Missionary Research Library in preparing the *North American Protestant Ministries Overseas Directory*, and is the manager of data collection and data processing for the next edition of the *World Christian Handbook*. MARC/DOC is a publication-distribution plan for missionary documentation that is either too small or too specific to be published in the usual channels. The Center also publishes a bi-monthly report on its projects that is distributed to about 7,000 individuals and organizations throughout the world.

In 1965 the Roman Catholic Church established in Washington, D.C., the Center for Applied Research in the Apostolate (CARA). CARA, like MARC, is goal-oriented; it engages in decision-oriented policy research as opposed to subject-oriented academic research. CARA is the only central research agency in the United States devoted to all aspects of the Catholic Church's mission in the contemporary world, both at home and overseas. Father Louis J. Luzbetak, S.V.D., the distinguished cultural anthropologist who serves as executive director of the Center, says, "We're promoting a cause, the mission of the church.... We are concerned with the utilization of knowledge — with steering practical knowledge through channels that will end up in action." CARA's overseas departments are the African Department, which is particularly strong in its documentation and information services, and the Oceania Department, which is still in its initial stage of development. The Center also conducts problem/project-oriented studies, such as the feasibility study it did on "A National Mission Training Institute," in which a model program for training U.S. Catholic overseas missionaries was developed. The Center publishes the findings of its various studies.

The most important resource in North America for research in the world mission of the church is the Missionary Research Library in New York City, of which Dr. Beaver was the director from 1948 to 1955. In 1967, due to inadequate support, the collections and equipment of the library were turned over to Union Theological Seminary, New York, which also assumed responsibility for the administration and maintenance of the library. The rich acquisitions program of the library continues, but the research and publications program, which now is the responsibility of the NCCC Division of Overseas Ministries, under the MRL name, has been greatly curtailed. Dr. Beaver has written about the disappointment of many scholars over the circumstances which brought this about:

> It was with the utmost optimism about support of the enterprise that the Missionary Research Library was created in 1914. The value of the services rendered through the years is incalculable. Yet adequate support has never been forthcoming from the mission boards or private foundations. It seems so logical to expect that a worldwide enterprise of the magnitude and complexity of the North

American world mission would find a recording, research, and survey agency absolutely indispensable and would give it high priority. That has not been the case. The M.R.L. has had to operate far more on the devotion and energy of its staff than on money.

The writer has never surrendered his hope that the mission boards will recognize the importance of providing cooperatively for themselves and for others the information, research and survey facility which is vitally necessary both for their individual and for ecumenical endeavors.[4]

There are vast resources and facilities for research in world mission, both Catholic and Protestant, throughout the world.[5]

---

[4] R. Pierce Beaver, "The Missionary Research Library, A Sketch of Its History," *Occasional Bulletin from the Missionary Research Library,* XIX, 2 (February 1968), 8. Cf. "Plans for the Future at the Missionary Research Library and for the *Occasional Bulletin,*" *ibid.,* XVII, 12 (December 1966), 1-2.

[5] For an indication of the extent of some of these resources, especially European and Roman Catholic, see the following: Livinus Vriens, *Critical Bibliography of Missiology,* vol. 2 in *"Bibliographia ad usum Seminariorum"* (Nijmegen: Bestelcentrale der V.S.K.B. Publ., 1930), 123 pp.; Angel Santos Hernandez, *Bibliografía Misional,* 2 vols. (Santander: Editorial Sal Terrae, 1965), 944 and 1299 pp.; Robert Streit and J. Dindinger, *Bibliotheca Missionum;* hrsg. von J. Rommerskirchen, N. Kowalsky, und J. Metzler; 26 vols. (published originally 1916ff.; reprinted and continued by Verlag Herder, Freiburg, 1963-68); Jos. Metzler, ed., *De Archivis et Bibliothecis Missionibus atque Scientiae Missionum inservientibus* (Rome: Pontificia Università Urbaniana de Propaganda Fide, 1968), 614 pp.; Josef Glazik, hrsg., *50 Jahre katholische Missionswissenschaft in Münster, 1911-1961* (Münster: Verlag Aschendorff, 1961), 212 pp.; Carol Van Arnhem and François Houtart, *Directory of Centers for Religious Research* (Louvain: FERES, International Federation of Institutes for Social and Socio-Religious Research, 1968), XII, 207 pp.; Frank W. Price, "Specialized Research Libraries in Missions," *Library Trends,* IX, 2 (October 1960), 175-85; Gerald H. Anderson, "Research Libraries in New York City Specializing in Christian Missions," *The Journal of Asian Studies,* XXV, 4 (August 1966), 733-36; James McCutcheon, "Missionary Archives in England for East and Southeast Asia: 1968, A Report," *ibid.,* XXVIII, 3 (May 1969), 601-02; Rosemary Keen, *Survey of Archives of Selected Missionary Societies* (London: Historical Manuscripts Commission, 1968); Leslie Ronald Marchant, *A Guide to the Archives and Records of Protestant Christian Missions from the British Isles to China, 1796-1914* (Nedlands, W.A.: University of Western Australia Press, 1966), XI, 134 pp.; A. C. Ross, "Manuscript Resources in the National Library of Scotland and the Library of the University of Edinburgh Relating to Christian Missions," *The Bulletin of the Scottish Institute of Missionary Studies,* No. 1 (June 1967), pp. 6-12; I. C. Cun-

But they are not supported, coordinated, and utilized adequately. The "plea for the promotion of missionary research through the creation of an international scientific institute for that purpose," expressed in 1951 by Dr. Olav G. Myklebust of the Egede Institute in Oslo, goes unmet, and its realization seems more remote than ever.[6]

At the same time as the MRL program was cut back in 1967, however, the Scottish Institute of Missionary Studies was founded. From very modest beginnings, with an editorial office at the University of Aberdeen, this new institute has shown remarkable initiative and vitality, especially in the areas of bibliographical services, and the locating and preserving of documentary materials. *The Bulletin* it publishes three times annually is devoted to a survey of current missionary literature, to information on archives, and to related concerns of the institute.

Also in 1967, *The Encyclopedia of Modern Christian Missions: The Agencies,* edited by Burton L. Goddard, was published under the aegis of the Gordon Divinity School in Massachusetts.[7] This is an authoritative source of information on the history, work, and administration of over fourteen hundred Protestant agencies, and as such would more properly be titled *A Handbook of Protestant Missionary Agencies.*

In 1971 the *Concise Dictionary of the Christian World Mission (1492-1969),* edited by Stephen C. Neill, John F. B. Goodwin, and Gerald H. Anderson, was published under the auspices of World Christian Books.[8] With over 900 articles on countries and regions, lives of missionaries and Christian thinkers, major

---

ningham, "A Further Deposit of Missionary Manuscripts in the National Library," *ibid.,* No. 2 (January 1968), pp. 3-4; John N. Schumacher and Gerald H. Anderson, "A Bibliographical Survey of Philippine Church History," *Studies in Philippine Church History* (Ithaca, N.Y.: Cornell University Press, 1969), pp. 389-412; John N. Sinclair, ed., "Location of archives of Protestant mission boards working in Latin America," *Protestantism in Latin America: A Bibliographical Guide* (Austin, Texas: The Hispanic American Institute, 1967), Appendix B, pp. 197-209; articles on "Archives," "Bibliographies," "Journals for Mission Studies," "Mission Libraries," "Mission Studies," "Research in Missions," in the *Concise Dictionary of the Christian World Mission* (London:. Lutterworth Press; and Nashville: Abingdon Press, 1971).

[6] Olav Guttorm Myklebust, *An International Institute of Scientific Missionary Research* (Oslo, 1951), p. 9.

[7] XIX (Camden, New Jersey, 1967).

[8] London and Nashville, 1970.

seminary agencies, and subjects ranging from acculturation to witchcraft, written by more than 200 contributors from every part of the church, the work is genuinely ecumenical and international. It is the first such comprehensive reference work on the Christian world mission since the publication of Edwin M. Bliss's *Encyclopaedia of Missions* in 1891 (revised in 1904), and it will probably be the last. The next such work will likely be an *Encyclopedia of World Christianity.*

"Missionary literature is to a large extent periodical literature."[9] A great many missionary periodicals are popular, promotional, and denominational, but there are also a good number of substantial, scholarly journals that provide a major channel for the publication of research in world mission. The premier English-language mission journal is the *International Review of Mission,* published quarterly since 1912 by the International Missionary Council and now by the Commission on World Mission and Evangelism of the World Council of Churches, Geneva.[10] Outstanding European Protestant journals are the *Evangelische Missions-Zeitschrift* (Hamburg), *Evangelisches Missions-Magazin* (Basel), *Frontier* (London), *De Heerbaan* (Amsterdam), *Nordisk Missions Tidsskrift* (Aarhus), *Norsk Tidsskrift for Misjon* (Oslo), and *Svensk Missionstidskrift* (Uppsala). Among the many notable Roman Catholic journals are *Eglise Vivante* (Louvain), *Misiones Extranjeras* (Burgos), *Het Missiewerk* (Nijmegen), *Neue Zeitschrift für Missionswissenschaft* (Beckenried), *Parole et Mission* (Paris), *Pro Mundi Vita* (Brussels), *Spiritus* (Paris), *Worldmission* (New York), and *Zeitschrift für Missionswissenschaft und Religionswissenschaft* (Münster). *Go Ye,* a quarterly magazine, is the organ of the Inter-Orthodox Missionary Center "Porefthendes" in Athens. It must be noted that no North American Protestant scholarly journal devoted to world mission is of the same standard as those mentioned above.

Some specialized journals related to mission studies are *Anthropos* (St. Augustin/Bonn), *Asia Focus* (Bangkok), *Bulletin of the Society for African Church History* (Aberdeen), *Cua-*

---

[9] John T. Ma, *Current Periodicals in the Missionary Research Library,* 2nd and rev. ed. (New York: MRL, 1961), p. 1. The MRL receives about 750 current periodicals.

[10] On the change of name from *International Review of Missions* to *International Review of Mission,* see "Editorial: Dropping the S," *IRM,* LVIII (April 1969), 141-44.

dernos Teológicos (Buenos Aires), *Indian Church History Review* (Serampore), *Indian Journal of Theology* (Serampore), *Japan Christian Quarterly* (Tokyo), *Japan Missionary Bulletin* (Tokyo), *Le Monde non Chrétien* (Paris), *Muslim World* (Hartford), *North East Asia Journal of Theology* (Tokyo), *Practical Anthropology* (Tarrytown, N.Y.), *Religion and Society* (Bangalore), *Rythmes du Monde* (Bruges), *South East Asia Journal of Theology* (Singapore), *Student World* (Geneva), and *Teaching All Nations* (Manila). Important also, in addition to the *Occasional Bulletin* from the MRL and *The Bulletin* of the Scottish Institute, are the *Church Growth Bulletin* (Pasadena) and the *Bulletin of Christian Institutes of Islamic Studies* (Lucknow).

There is as yet no Protestant equivalent to the annual *Bibliografia Missionaria,* edited in Rome by Giovanni Rommerskirchen, O.M.I. Some scholars feel it would be helpful if the *International Review of Mission* would publish its "Bibliography on World Mission and Evangelism" in expanded form as a special fifth number of the *IRM* each year, rather than in the present quarterly fashion, and thereby create in one convenient issue an annual bibliography, similar to that of the Dutch Catholic journal *Het Missiewerk.*

Research and writing in world mission are carried on primarily by professional mission scholars, represented among Protestants especially in the membership of such professional organizations as the Association of Professors of Missions in North America and the Deutsche Gesellschaft für Missionswissenschaft. A conference of Anglo-European missiologists has developed, with meetings at Birmingham in 1968 and at Oslo in 1970. Increasingly important also are the research and writing done by mission scholars, both missionaries and nationals, in Asia, Oceania, Africa, and Latin America, and the formation of scholarly societies to encourage and support their work. One such professional organization is the Southeast Asia Society of Church History and Ecumenics, formed at Hong Kong in 1968, of which Dr. Beaver is the honorary president. Roman Catholic mission studies have been greatly stimulated by the annual mission weeks in Louvain, Milan, Burgos, Freiburg (Switzerland), and elsewhere, the papers from which are usually published.

A development of significance, pointed out by Dr. Beaver, is that "most writing in the history of missions is not being done by church historians, but by general historians and area experts in the universities and colleges who have recently discovered the importance of the Christian mission in international relations and in intercultural exchange."[11] This will increasingly be the case as the number of missiologists declines.

What are some of the more urgent issues and questions that need to be taken up by mission scholars today? Dr. Beaver, speaking to this point in his address at the first Anglo-European consultation on mission studies at Selly Oak Colleges, Birmingham, in 1968, said:

> The great task and major role of missiology today is to clarify and define for a confused and lukewarm church the meaning of mission in an age which is both ecumenical and secular.... The second principal role or task ought to be the assumption of leadership in the new ecumenism, guiding the churches constructively and creatively in mission towards that unity already given in Christ. The ecumenical movement came out of the mission to the nations, and the new ecumenism which includes Rome can well be given direction and inspiration by missiology.

Dr. Beaver defined these tasks further:

> As missiology attempts to play these two roles or carry out these two tasks, the major problems with which it must wrestle are these: the relationship between Christian faith and other religions, the relationship between faith and culture, and the relationship between discipling of the

---

[11] "Editorial Foreword," *Mo Bradley and Thailand* by Donald C. Lord (Grand Rapids, Mich., 1969), p. 7. An example of this is the field of Asian history at Harvard University where doctoral candidates are directed for research to the archives of the American Board of Commissioners for Foreign Missions, which are deposited in the Treasure Room (Houghton) of the Harvard College Library. Dr. Beaver has also pointed out that nearly all the articles relating to missions now received by the journal *Church History* are submitted by general historians, and the great majority of members of the American Society of Church History are not church historians in the seminaries, but are rather college and university professors who are interested in religion as a factor in history.

nations and discipling the nation, or between the world-wide sending mission and local evangelism.[12]

Several related issues also require the attention of missiologists in the days ahead. For instance, there is the dilemma created by the opposition of "Christian presence" to "Christian proclamation." There is the polarity between evangelism and social justice, between mission and service, and between conversion and dialogue. And there is the need to define and describe more adequately the distinctions between mission, witness, and evangelism.[13]

Books that study the style and shape of the Christian life and faith on non-Western soil will be of particular interest and importance in the days ahead. These would best be written by nationals of these regions, but missionaries will have much to

----

[12] "The Meaning and Place of Missiology Today in the American Scene," Selly Oak Colleges European Consultation on Mission Studies, April 1968, pp. 7-8, mimeographed. Willem A. Bijlefeld, discussing the relationship of Christians to men of other faiths, says: "The crucial point for Protestants and Roman Catholics alike is indeed this one: do we dare to face and discuss honestly and openly the question whether there is still *any* place for the church as a particular social entity and a separate religious community in an environment conditioned and to a large extent determined by another cultural and religious tradition than Christianity? . . . As long as we stress the need of a transformation from within one religious community into another, we are still dealing with 'continuity or discontinuity.' . . . The plea for proclaiming the Gospel not only initially, but as a permanent structure 'within Hindu (Muslim, Buddhist) cul'ure and religion' is the only real move beyond Tambaram 1938 of which I know" ("Trends in the Contemporary Discussion on 'Christians and Men of Other Faiths,'" *The Hartford Quarterly,* VIII, 3 [1968], 54-55). The plea to which Bijlefeld refers was that by Kaj Baago in "The Post-Colonial Crisis of Missions," *International Review of Mission,* LV, 219 (July 1966), 322-32 and LVI, 221 (January 1967), 99-103.

[13] Several numbers of the *International Review of Mission* and *The Ecumenical Review* have been devoted in recent years to discussion of these issues.

When Karl Barth was once asked, "What is the difference between a missionary, a witness, and an evangelist?" he answered, "You speak of a missionary in relation to God's mission to and in the world. You speak of a witness in relation to the signs and tokens of the Kingdom. An evangelist is a person whom D. T. Niles invented." When D. T. Niles later asked Barth what he meant by this, Barth laughed and said, "I don't like the word 'evangelist.' The word seems to me to suggest that evangelism is a talking activity" (D. T. Niles, "Karl Barth — A Personal Memory," *The South East Asia Journal of Theology,* XI [Autumn 1969], 11).

contribute here as well.[14] There is a continuing need for the tools of missionary scholarship: bibliographies, directories, and surveys of research.

Mr. Calvin P. Bulthuis, vice-president and editor of the William B. Eerdmans Publishing Company, says that the publication of mission studies may be divided roughly into three categories.

> The first consists of quite popular works, usually dramatic personal experiences of contemporary missionaries or popular biographies of denominational missionary heroes. The second consists of that broad middle range between popular and scholarly — secondary and tertiary studies designed for use in seminaries and by the serious lay student of missions. The third consists of rather thoroughgoing and definitive studies — historical, methodological, and theological — which the better libraries stock and the scholars of missions use for resources in their teaching.[15]

Books in the first category often tend toward sentimental missionary hagiography, which is unfortunate because, as Mr. Bulthuis says, "good popular books on the cause of missions can feed the very people who over the years have been traditionally so very faithful in supporting missionaries and missions." Three good examples of the second category are the "Christian World Mission Books," edited by Dr. Beaver for Eerdmans, the William Carey Library, which is a series of semi-technical mission books

---

[14] Commendable contributions in this direction are the series "Confessing the Faith in India," published by the Christian Literature Society, Madras, in cooperation with the Christian Institute for the Study of Religion and Society in Bangalore; the series "Theologische Stimmen aus Asien, Afrika und Lateinamerika," published by Chr. Kaiser Verlag, Munich; the World Council of Churches series "World Studies of Churches in Mission," published by Lutterworth Press, London; and "Die Kirchen der Welt" series (Reihe B.), published by Evangelisches Verlagswerk, Stuttgart.

Bishop Stephen Neill has pointed out that "Christian history has been written far too much from the side of the operators and far too little from that of the victims. . . . We know fairly well what it feels like to be a missionary; we know much less of what it feels like to be the object of the missionary's attentions. What is the process through which the Gospel becomes first intelligible, then attractive, and finally overwhelming in its demands?" ("The History of Missions: An Academic Discipline," *The Mission of the Church and the Propagation of the Faith,* ed. G. J. Cuming [London, 1970], p. 160).

[15] Letter to the writer, February 6, 1970.

published in South Pasadena, California, and the "Weltmission heute" series, published by the Evangelischer Missionsverlag, Stuttgart. Major examples of the third category are the "Missionswissenschaftliche Forschungen" series sponsored by the Deutsche Gesellschaft für Missionswissenschaft and published by Gütersloher Verlagshaus Gerd Mohn, the "Studia Missionalia Upsaliensia" series published by Gleerups, Lund, the "World Mission Studies" published by SCM Press, London, and the "Missionswissenschaftliche Abhandlungen und Texte" series sponsored by the Internationales Institut für Missionswissenschaftliche Forschungen in Münster and published by Verlag Aschendorff, Münster.

In this period of confusion and transition in world mission, says Dr. Beaver, "the missiologist is called to be the pioneer and to blaze the trail. The missionary will not escape from his uncertainty until the missiologist points the way, and the church will not move ahead in mission unless the missiologist sounds a prophetic call."[16] Out of his research and writing, and through his published works, the missiologist today has an unparalleled opportunity and responsibility to serve the future of the Christian world mission.

---

[16] "The Meaning and Place of Missiology Today in the American Scene," p. 10.

JAMES A. SCHERER, a pastor of the Lutheran Church in America, is Professor of World Mission at the Lutheran School of Theology at Chicago. From 1957 to 1969 he served as Dean of the Lutheran School of Missions, a pre-field training program with which Dr. Beaver was associated on a number of occasions as guest instructor. Mr. Scherer was a teacher for the Yale-in-China Association in Changsha, Hunan, from 1946-49, and served as a missionary evangelist for the Japan Evangelical Lutheran Church from 1952 to 1956. A graduate of Yale University, he received his doctorate from Union Theological Seminary in New York. He has also studied at Oxford University and at the Tokyo International Christian University. He is the author of *Missionary, Go Home!, Mission and Unity in Lutheranism,* and *Justinian Welz,* and has contributed to five other books.

10

James A. Scherer: Missions in Theological Education

FORECASTING THE FUTURE OF WORLD MISSIONS IN THEOLOGICAL education is a hazardous task fraught with the same pitfalls as predicting the future of the organized church. The prophet is likely to be more rash than right. A responsible observer — one not bent on making headlines — would wisely stop after making some cautious observations on the nature of the changes in progress. He would be keenly conscious that the whole theological scene is in a state of ferment, and that today's trends do not necessarily augur tomorrow's realities. He would stop short of making firm predictions. Yet he might venture to record some random observations after reflecting on the meaning of over a century of teaching world missions as a part of theological education. From such reflections there might emerge a few accurate indications of the future.

I. RETROSPECT

He who would prophesy the future should have a long historical memory. As that indefatigable researcher of the history of our subject O. G. Myklebust has shown, the struggle to gain recognition for world missions within the theological curriculum has been a long, uphill battle.[1] The fortunes of mission education parallel and reflect those of the missionary enterprise itself.

---

[1] O. G. Myklebust, *The Study of Missions in Theological Education*, I (Oslo, 1955), II (1957).

It is sobering to recall that world missions is a comparative newcomer to theological education, being barely a century old. The venerable guardians of the portals of theological education still tend to regard missiology as an upstart and an intruder, having no rightful place alongside the established disciplines. It lacks antiquity, some say, since it is not found in the classical theological encyclopedia. It is superfluous, others add, for its concerns are already dealt with by the major theological disciplines. It is anachronistic, still others complain, now that the age of missions is over. Whatever the attitude, it can be safely asserted that world missions has not yet found a secure place in the theological curriculum. The teaching of world missions gained access to the court of the gentiles, but it could not find admittance to the inner sanctum of theological study!

The year 1867, Myklebust observes, was a decisive year for the breakthrough of mission instruction into the curriculum of Protestant theological schools: Alexander Duff began his work as Professor of Evangelistic Theology at New College, Edinburgh; Carl Plath launched an ambitious scheme to establish chairs of missions in German universities; and Rufus Anderson, pioneer American mission theorist, began delivering his peripatetic lectures on "Foreign Missions: Their Relations and Claims" at Andover and other Eastern seminaries.[2] Three regular professorships of missions and a few scattered lectureships constituted the sum total of mission instruction in American theological schools around the turn of the century. In the wake of the Edinburgh Conference of 1910, however, and particularly during the 1920's and 1930's, most American schools added full or part-time professorships of world missions, and offered at least one required course in the field. World missions was generally regarded as a subhead of practical theology, though occasionally it was designated the co-responsibility of the professor of church history or world religions. It was commonly viewed as a mere appendage to theological study, and its proper con-

---

[2] *Ibid.*, I, 25-26. Carl Graul, retired director of the Leipzig Mission, had delivered his habilitation lecture on missions at Erlangen University as early as 1864, but his untimely death prevented him from embarking on his planned lectureship. Warneck's chair of missions at Halle was not established until 1897. Duff's chair ranks as the first endowed chair of missions in a university-related faculty of theology.

tent and relation to older theological disciplines were never clarified.

The beginnings of world missions instruction were plagued by a certain immaturity and obscurity with regard to definition, methodological basis, and objectives. In retrospect, it appears that the credibility of the claims of world missions to a rightful place in theological education was weakened by a failure to think through the nature and requirements of the infant discipline and the manner in which these were to be represented in the curriculum. Was world missions merely an appendage to ecclesiology or practical theology, and therefore capable of being dealt with in a facts and methods course? Or did world missions have a solid theoretical and methodological basis which allowed it to challenge and to interact with other disciplines? What were the aims of the new subject? Were they related primarily to motivation and training, or did they have basic theological understanding as their object? The lack of an early consensus in these matters is reflected in the divergences between the continental European and the North American approaches to the teaching of world missions.

The Germans in particular, and the Dutch and Scandinavians to a lesser extent, sought to make missiology an exact science that could be studied as a detached subject at the university. "Missionswissenschaft," it was argued, deserved public recognition because of its relevance to general knowledge, its scientific foundation, and its academic methodology. Gustav Warneck's five-volume *Evangelische Missionslehre* represents the classic exposition of this viewpoint. The object was to gain theological respectability and prestige for missiology by establishing regular university professorships in the subject and demanding that missiology be included in the list of required lectures and examination subjects. This view assumes that what is not recognized as a valid academic subject carries no prestige and will not be taken seriously. One must understand that evangelical missionary work on the continent was carried out as an activity of private mission societies without benefit of recognition by state churches or leading faculties of theology.

The American view, with the notable exception of Rufus Anderson, was influenced almost entirely by pragmatic considerations. As with Duff's professorship in Scotland, support for

145

mission teaching in American seminaries grew out of the conviction that an activity which was enjoying increasing popularity in the churches themselves should also be reflected in training for the ministry. Missionary education was included in pastoral training for two reasons: (1) to provide a modicum of pre-field training for would-be missionary candidates, and (2) to foster missionary support at the local level by encouraging future pastors to take the leadership in missionary promotion. This approach was largely shaped by the methods of the Student Volunteer Movement to nurture missionary commitment. A pastor's missionary manual from 1895 states that "it should be the supreme desire and effort of every pastor that from his church . . . should go rank after rank of new recruits for the conquest of the world for Christ"; moreover, ministers were "to create and maintain an intelligent, sympathetic, active interest in foreign missions among the students who . . . remain in the home field, in order to secure the strong backing of this great enterprise by men and money."[3] In America, the motivational and promotional aspects of missionary education clearly took precedence over the scholarly, scientific aspects.

The continental viewpoint, emphasizing missiology as an autonomous academic discipline, tended to divorce the subject matter of mission study from church life and practice and to relate it to the concerns of the university. Its strength lay in the careful development of methodological clarity and investigative procedures, in which the sources of study and the findings were correlated with other branches of learning. Missiology proper, linguistic and cultural analysis, and the history of religions have been enormously enriched by this continental contribution. Training for missiology is more rigorously developed on the continent than elsewhere, and literature on the subject traditionally reflects greater analytical depth and precision than do most similar Anglo-Saxon studies. American missiology, by contrast, has been generally immature and underdeveloped with reference to training, research methods, and scholarly publications. Its strength has been in its church-relatedness, but its weaknesses grew out of the fact that the instruction had a marked promotional flavor, lacked critical method, and was usually given by an amateur who specialized in something else.

---

[3] J. E. Adams, *The Missionary Pastor* (New York, 1895), pp. 3-4.

Recently the cleavage between the two approaches has been narrowed. American training and standards of missiology have become more demanding, and missionary work on the continent has become more closely related to the life of the churches.

A second issue that has impeded the growth and maturity of world missions in theological education has been the disagreement over educational philosophies. The two alternative viewpoints may be described as "permeation" (or integration) and "concentration" (or specialization). The most ardent advocates of permeation are found in the British Isles, where theological educators staunchly hold that no special provision for world missions is needed apart from occasional lectureships. When biblical studies, patristics, church history, ecclesiology, and pastoralia are properly taught, so the argument runs, the missionary emphasis will be adequately represented. Britain has only one active professorship of world missions (at Selly Oak Colleges), and his work is largely related to the actual preparation of missionary candidates.[4] In Britain the real missiologists tend to be missionary administrators like Max Warren. Advocates of concentration are of course found in the dozen or more Protestant theological faculties on the continent possessing regular mission professorships. Here missiology is taught as a specialized discipline alongside other specialized disciplines. Mission study reaches a greater level of depth and concentration but affects only a limited number of students.

The American solution has been instinctively wiser. American theological schools, after wavering between the two alternatives, have generally opted for both: permeation and concentration, integration and specialization.[5] There are those who believe that the missionary cause is best served when the regular theological disciplines devote significant attention to mission perspectives: for example, biblical theology by establishing the necessary foundation and eschatological framework; church history by delineating the worldwide expansion of the church and calling attention to pertinent missionary lessons from church history; and systematic theology by providing the necessary analytical tools for the apologetic encounter with the world of religions, cultures, and social change. Yet this view is not incompatible

---

4 Myklebust, II, 45.
5 *Ibid.*, p. 64.

with the belief that specific courses dealing with the life and growth of churches in Asia, Africa, and Latin America, or with the problems arising from the encounter between the gospel and other religions, cultures, and ideologies, should also be available. The Edinburgh Conference (1910) went so far as to recommend that some prescribed course in world missions form an integral part of the curriculum of every theological school. It also urged that special endowments be raised for world mission lectureships, that mission collections in theological libraries be enlarged, and that voluntary mission study groups be organized in schools.[6] World missions in American theological education has tended to follow this pluralistic approach.

What have been the results of these several endeavors? It would appear that those who argued for separate chairs of mission were right in their contention that the missionary emphasis would, at best, always tend to remain marginal in the major theological disciplines. "The church is mission," recent ecclesiology declares; yet "what is everybody's business becomes nobody's business." The same logic which led to the establishment of special mission structures and agencies also dictates that missionary activity be represented, at least in part, by means of special instruction. The proliferation of study materials and the tendency toward specialization in all disciplines make a similar concentration on missiological studies inevitable. Mission studies remain infantile and amateurish unless given the opportunity to pursue their own lines of development to the fullest extent. Desirable as it may be that the mission emphasis be affirmed in the curriculum as a whole, world missions also needs specific points of focus to give it greater visibility on the theological horizon. These are studies in the life and growth patterns of overseas churches, strategies and structures which permit the church to communicate the gospel across the frontiers of language, culture, and religion, the movement toward mission in unity, and so on. The sense of mission is best conveyed when theological interpretation is firmly linked with concrete historical reality.

On the other hand, it must be candidly admitted that the high hopes held for professorships of world missions have not been altogether realized. Those who thought that adding mis-

---

[6] *World Missionary Conference* (1910), VI, 179 ff.

sions courses to the theological curriculum would automatically help maintain missionary vigor in the church must feel some disappointment. No comparable forward thrust in missionary outreach appears to have followed the introduction of special missionary education, though undoubtedly there has been some overall gain in the consolidation of institutional support. The greatest periods of missionary advance, in point of fact, came at times when the missionary cause had no theological recognition. The missions of the Moravians, of Halle pietism, and of the evangelical awakening of the late eighteenth and early nineteenth centuries, and the mighty flood of missionary volunteers in the late 1880's and 1890's were accomplished mostly without the recognition of either church or theological establishment. The case of Alexander Duff shows that a brilliant churchman and an eminently qualified professor of missions cannot through academic channels alone inspire students to missionary commitment. Such commitment is always prior to theology and rests upon the more immediate foundation of faith and apostolic obedience. Theology in the service of the missionary task may clarify goals and motives; it may provide valuable lessons from church history; and it may help to correlate strategies and methods to existing conditions. Theology, in short, can serve as a corrective to missionary arbitrariness and onesidedness. But it cannot, in the nature of the case, motivate to missionary action.

Mission and evangelism are activities from *faith* to *faith*. Theology cannot supply the deficiency of vital faith and missionary spirit, but it can guide faith seeking mature expression into missionary obedience that is intelligent (*fides quaerens intellectum*). The missionary volunteers understood that obedience was always a matter of personal commitment. They fostered that commitment through voluntary study groups and prayer fellowships. They did not suppose that the missionary vision could be imparted primarily through missionary instruction or mere commitment to institutional missionary goals. The vision was caught, not taught. In time, however, the fervor of the early volunteers waned, and missionary instruction in seminaries came to have a more institutionalized character. It became part of the education of the well-rounded churchman, and served to guide persons contemplating missionary careers. It could convey information and stimulate interest, but it could not be expected to carry the burden of awakening commitment. It was also obliged to adhere more and more to established academic norms. This change in the nature of missionary education in American seminaries raises important questions. What goals are valid for teaching world missions today? How can these goals best be reached?

II. PROSPECT

In looking to the future we may now venture to make three brief programmatic suggestions for the discipline of world missions as a part of theological education in North America: (1) world missions must establish itself on a firmer footing; (2) it must continually redefine its own meaning and relevance; and (3) it must be prepared to serve sacrificially.

1. World missions must establish itself on a firmer footing. We have noted that immaturity and lack of a solid foundation tended to frustrate the entry of mission study into the inner courts of theology. Missiology has, with some justice, claimed the whole realm of learning and culture as its proper subject, but it has not always made good that gigantic claim. It must strive for the broadest possible correlation between the missionary motive and intention, on the one hand, and the disciplines of theology and secular learning, on the other. But it must do so in the full awareness that its right to be present in the halls of learning will be disputed by many.

Mission relates itself to humanity, to the world of nations, and to the realms of knowledge and culture not as a neutral analyst or objective observer but as an *advocate* and special *pleader*. Missiology wants to know and understand in order to change and influence — to bring all things into subjection to the Lordship of Jesus Christ. Its right to be present in the academic world will depend solely upon its competence, for it cannot be admitted on the basis of its motives. Thus missiology is obliged to strive for mastery over the areas of knowledge which especially concern it, even though in the nature of the case it will fall short of total systematization.

As the missionary must be all things to all men in order to save some (I Cor. 9:22), so missiology must be distinguished by its versatility and adaptability in relating to knowledge and issues. Its presence among other disciplines will be dialogical and attentive, provocative and responsive. It will assist and support sister disciplines as well as the church in erecting signs of the Kingdom in the world. It should strive to be the most charismatic of all disciplines, at once confident of its own validity and urgency, but flexible and humble enough to learn from all.

In order to do this, missiology must enter more fully into dialogue between the missionary task, theology, and learning:

a. The would-be professor of world missions should be fully trained in one of the major disciplines, such as church history, systematic theology, or the history of religions. He should also have an active interest in history, the social sciences, international relations, and various other disciplines related to the practice of world missions.

b. He should have the benefit of practical field-work in a mission situation, including firsthand observation of and participation in the life of a non-Christian population, where the methodologies of evangelism, church development, and cross-cultural communication are tested. Since the time of Graul, the mission situation has been an important school for missiologists.

c. He should be continuously related in some way to the actual missionary work of the church, at home or abroad — for example, by means of a liaison with boards and agencies for mission, or direct participation in a mission project. In this way he will be kept abreast of changing issues and needs.

d. He should be engaged in a dialogue with colleagues in other theological disciplines and in the secular fields in order to interpret the missionary task to them as well as to receive insights from their disciplines that may be of special value for missionary education and practice.

2. World missions must continually redefine its meaning and relevance, both in terms of theory and practice. Missionary work has been plagued by outmoded popular images from an earlier colonial era that no longer fit the situation. Resources have been tied down in long-term "trench warfare" due to a lack of func-

tional mobility. Concepts and strategies have more often been responses to social and political changes than forerunners of such changes. In these respects mission work today cannot be done without clearly defined goals and projections into the future that are based on historical realities. It is the task of missiology to redefine these goals in terms of the needs of each age and place, and then to interpret them to mission administrators, theologians, and churchmen in general. In doing so, missiology must be aware of the need to maintain historical continuity in the midst of the discontinuities of history. What are the permanently valid criteria for mission? Alternatively, what changes of form, content, and method are permissible without denying the original missionary mandate? Posing such theoretical questions and then correlating theory and practice should be the concern of missiology.

Within the century since world missions was initiated as an infant theological discipline, missionary practice has undergone major transitions. Early missions were concerned with evangelism, gospel-preaching, and conversion. Missionary instruction was then largely occupied with evangelistic methods and problems of recruitment and support. Soon came the period of church-centric missions. Classroom teaching now reflected the goals of church-planting — the "three-self" marks of independence, the training of native workers, stewardship, and the challenges of cooperation and unity. During the 1940's and 1950's came colossal changes in former colonial territories — issues of new nationhood, revivals in ancient religions, and upheavals in our Western theological certainties. These demanded not merely a reappraisal of older assumptions and relationships, but a thorough search for a valid continuing basis for world missions. We are still in the midst of that discussion. More recently the church-centric preoccupation has given way to newer theological interpretations with a conspicuous missionary interest. These seek to explore the immediate impact of the Kingdom upon the world and history in all its diversity and complexity. Missiology must concern itself with the various theologies of hope, the future, revolution, and universalism, carefully sifting chaff from wheat and giving its own witness to the permanent relevance of the great commission.

3. World missions must be prepared to serve sacrificially, with-

out recognition or reward. I have already indicated that the teaching of world missions has not, except in periods of a popular missionary tide, been a subject of great popularity with theologians and seminary students. Nevertheless, world missions has an essential function as the handmaid of theology and the church. If mission is the enduring purpose of the church, then missiology must also be an integral and authentic component of theological education. Yet the history of Israel, as well as that of the church, demonstrates that the people of God are time and again tempted to deny or to forget their missionary calling. World missions reminds theology of the eschatological dimensions beyond church history and tradition. It recalls the church to her proper vocation of going beyond her own parochial life to be the witness and bearer of salvation to the world. Missiology plays its part by insisting that the church, in the midst of change and decay all around, maintain continuity with Christ and the disciples in its most essential apostolic task. Among all of the disciplines of theology, a place of honor is reserved for this humble servant in the master's house, for it has been good and faithful in the duties entrusted to it.

WILLIAM J. DANKER, Professor of Missions at Concordia Seminary at St. Louis since 1956, graduated from Concordia and served as a pastor in northern Illinois. He is the founder of the Japan Lutheran Church and was a missionary in that country from 1948 to 1956. He did graduate work at Wheaton College, the University of Chicago, and Heidelberg University, where he earned his Th.D. writing under Professor Hans-Werner Gensichen. He was a visiting professor at Heidelberg University from 1966 to 1967 and at Luther Seminary, St. Paul, in 1968. He is the author of *Two Worlds or None* and *Profit for the Lord,* and is the editor of the Witnessing Church Series published by Concordia Publishing House and the Church-in-Mission Series published by Fortress Press.

11

William J. Danker: A Piece of the Action: A New Economic Basis for the Church

D URING THE 1960's URBAN MISSIONARIES LEARNED TO CHANT the litany that the church must "go where the action is." However, empty-handed kibitzers rarely discover an effective role. The church talks about entering the power structure, but it fails to act on the principle that economic power is basic.

During a recent study tour of East Asia it became clear to me that the church there is not content merely to go where the action is. It intends to play a role. *It wants a piece of the action.*

There is a new vertical world rising out of the once horizontal skyline of Asian cities. Farsighted national leaders know that if the church is to have any part in these cities tomorrow it must have a piece of the action today.

Tokyo has changed twice as much in the past seven years as it did in the previous seven-year span. Returning to the city where I served as a postwar missionary, I felt like an *O-nobori-san* — a country peasant gawking in the big city — amid the maze of elevated highways and new buildings and the flood of Japanese autos. Only seven years ago buildings in Tokyo were limited to nine stories because of earthquakes. But canny Japanese engineers solved that problem and calmly erected the Kasumigaseki Building of thirty-six stories deliberately made to whiplash rather than break. Hardly pausing to gloat, they went on to build a number of structures with more than forty stories. This represents an addition of up to 400 per cent more vertical Tokyo in strategic sections of this megalopolis of 11.8 million people. It means the skyrocketing of land prices in this largest city in human history, where sites for conventional church buildings are increasingly priced far beyond the church's reach.

The same process is gathering momentum in Seoul, Korea. When I was there seven years ago, the tallest building was seven stories. Now it is twenty-four stories.

This soaring vertical world confronts an Asian church that is generally small and poor. And the shape of the church brought from Europe and America usually fits Asian society rather poorly.

But a new spirit is stirring. Churchmen are finding independent solutions. Already in Hawaii, where America blends into Asia, a very significant instance has come into view. The Prince of Peace Lutheran Church in the Waikiki area of Honolulu is a church in the new vertical idiom. This "penthouse church" occupies the twelfth and thirteenth stories of a tall apartment building rented out to senior citizens. The church pays taxes on the commercial portion of the structure. The pastor's office is on the ground floor accessible to any passerby. The church got nowhere in the Waikiki hotel area until it hit upon this vertical, commercial approach. But for two years the struggle was waged in the highest councils of its denomination. Laymen, particularly, contended that "the church should not go into business."

On the hillside campus of Taiwan Theological Seminary, overlooking the prosperous city of Taipei, rental apartments provide one-third of the annual budget of this thriving Presbyterian school. In Seoul the Korea Lutheran Mission maintains its headquarters in the five-story Jedong Building, a short distance from the city hall and the national capitol. Space not needed by the church is rented to commercial firms. Acquired in 1962, the building is now expected to pay for itself by 1972 and should produce significant revenue thereafter for missions and Christian social welfare work. Han Guk Theological Seminary is erecting a ten- to twelve-story office building in downtown Seoul. This is the chief asset of a foundation expected to provide the entire operating expenses of the school. Interdenominational Central Theological Seminary has no supporting mission boards overseas. But it owns one of the most strategic sections in Seoul's "mile-long building," an eight-story, one-kilometer-long arcade of stores and apartments. Determined to be the church in the world and train its students for Christian witness in the world, the seminary holds its classes there.

Visitors to Expo '70 in Osaka found few churches in the heart of this dynamic mercantile city. One exception is the Higashi-Umeda church of Japan's leading Protestant denomination, the Nihon Kirisuto Kyodan. Ten minutes' walk from Umeda central station, a cross looms on a nine-story office building, and in the well-appointed, ninth-floor church sanctuary on the Sunday before Christmas, I heard a youthful choir singing Handel's *Hallelujah Chorus* above a hard-nosed business city: "The kingdoms of this world shall become the Kingdom of our Lord and of His Christ." Built in 1965 and financed entirely in Japan, the structure is expected to pay for itself by 1976. The 280-member church, which supports a full-time staff of five, including three pastors, has pledged itself not to use any profits for itself. They are to be devoted to mission and Christian welfare work.

Not far away, the Bishop of Kyoto's Episcopal diocese has his offices in the attractive Palace-Side Hotel, constructed by a devoted Episcopal layman on land owned by the church. After fifteen years the entire building becomes the property of the church without cost. Meanwhile, the bishop has use of a hotel room for his guests as well as a meeting room for diocesan purposes. The same Japanese businessman stimulated the diocese to another, even larger enterprise. St. John's Episcopal Church borrowed government funds with which to develop its strategic Kyoto site. Next to its new church building it erected a ten-story apartment complex containing ninety-five dwelling units and a supermarket. The pastor finds it far easier to approach people for witness and ministry here than in a more conventional church removed from society.

Asia offers many other opportunities for getting a piece of the action. There is a crying need for capital in the volatile, inflated economy of the Philippines. In Korea even the government charges 30 per cent interest per annum on loans, while loan sharks charge 120 per cent. The cautiously invested pension fund of a large American firm in the Philippines earned 35 per cent in 1967 in a large Manila bank's investment trust department.

Nor need the action always be capitalistic and profit-making. In Kyoto, Masao Takenaka, professor of Christian ethics at Doshisha University, is persuading a large labor union to gradually assume the full salary of a popular Christian pastor who heads the union's educational and cultural program.

Some of the reasons why Asian churchmen are striving to get a piece of the action are the following:

1. *Vertical urbanization.* Horizontal, agrarian, parochial forms of church structure and support will not meet the demands of the new upright dimension.

2. *Full-orbed stewardship.* One great asset of otherwise economically weak Asian churches is the strategically placed land they acquired in the past. Even within the last twenty years the value of the property has sometimes risen as much as a hundred times. The safe and sometimes cowardly course is to sell these irreplaceable plots and build a church painlessly elsewhere from the profits. But the churches can find an ongoing indigenous flow of income if they engage in the more risky process of developing such properties.

One Asian church affiliated with a large American denomination owns downtown property in an Asian capital worth several million dollars. But the American mission board has invested its assets of over $100 million elsewhere. Meanwhile, the Asian real estate develops no income for the church and no taxes for the city, and it makes no addition to the country's economic development. And well-trained young pastors of that denomination receive a salary of less than $30 per month, forcing many to leave the ministry.

Another church affiliated with a large American denomination was forced to sell its priceless downtown property because it lacked the capital to develop it. While U.S. churches with their large memberships may be able to afford such folly, for the tiny churches of Asia, selling such urban real estate may be suicide.

3. *A desire to get out of the ecclesiastical ghetto and into the secular world.* From Professor Takenaka to humble pastors and unknown laymen, the church in Asia feels the need of what Dr. Jacques Rossel, director of the Basel Mission Society, calls *Reibungsfläche,* a surface of encounter with the world. The Christians of Asia have comparatively few problems on the

question of getting a piece of the action. It is significant that the impetus is generally coming from them. Most American mission boards still seem to be trailing far behind the thinking of pioneering Asian church leaders.

4. A *strong desire for an indigenous, independent economic base for the churches of Asia.* In *The Economic Basis of the Church,* a report volume which received far less attention than it deserved at the 1938 assembly of the International Missionary Council at Madras, J. Merle Davis quotes the Karens of Burma saying, "If we eat our own rice, we can do things our own way." Reflecting this just spirit of independence, Professor Takenaka insisted on raising three-fourths of the cost of Seminar House, an evangelical academy-type operation near Kyoto. But few church-related projects will qualify for the substantial help he recruited from non-Christian Japanese industrial leaders.

Asian cities are a fast-moving, televised, air-conditioned, neon-lighted blur. Japan builds bullet trains streaking at 130 mph between Tokyo and Osaka. It builds the largest ships in the world and is planning tankers of more than 500,000 tons. A projected new train could cover the entire length of Japan in three to five hours on a cushion of air. In this kind of "can do" society Christians are soul-weary of any remnants of fiscal dependence on the West, especially when the means of obtaining freedom are ready to hand. Asians are tired of ramshackle mission chapels when the societies they live in, including the new religions, are going first class. An indigenous economic base is a prerequisite for the flowering of an indigenous theology and an Asian style of church life.

Many objections will leap to the mind of the Western Christian. Space will not allow me to deal with them adequately here, but I should like to briefly respond to a few.

1. *Won't the Asian spiritual mentality be offended by religion's entry into commerce?*

There is a certain compartmentalization of the sacred and the profane in Asian religions. Ordinarily, this can be satisfied by setting up separate organizational structures to take care of business affairs. Even transcendental Hinduism is supported by real estate holdings of the Hindu Temple Fund, a fund so vast that it is administered under the supervision of the Indian government. Muslim mosques are maintained by the *waq'f* foundation system. Professor Takenaka sees nothing wrong with the Episcopal hotel and apartment house in Kyoto. He terms this approach "sensible." The pastor of the church which built the apartment house said that while some people have thought it strange, intellectuals and professional people see nothing to criticize.

2. *Will stewardship be adversely affected?*

It need not be. A realistic stewardship of brains, land, and opportunity could represent a more developed kind of stewardship. Adequate resources could, in fact, encourage stewardship, which often gives up in the face of a seemingly impossible task. The tremendous challenges faced by the small Asian churches — especially in their efforts to be independent of the West — ought to keep them from letting up on individual offerings in spite of any supplementary commercial income.

3. *Won't the church become too rich and powerful for the rest of society?*

Not the tiny churches of Asia and not in the face of the headstart already gained by the rest of the corporate economy. The history of the church in some parts of Europe should not be projected onto Asia's totally different situation.

4. *Will the church evade taxes?*

Asian laws generally won't allow it. The commercial stewardship of resources would allow the church to pay taxes without dipping into its own inadequate offerings. In this respect, the legal situation in Asia is generally better than the situation in the United States described by Alfred Balk in *The Religion Business,* an analysis which does not apply to the Asian context. In this way the church can satisfy its obligations both to God and to Caesar.

5. *Is it safe to proceed on a course of commercial development in the face of strong Asian family loyalties?*

If there is serious uncertainty on this score, perhaps the wiser course may be to engage real estate development or management firms, if possible. Counsel may be sought from secular commercial firms which operate successfully in the same social ambience.

6. *Won't Asian churches compromise their Christian witness by entering a capitalistic system? Isn't Black Power indicting*

American churches for precisely such a compromise — for profit-ing from an unjust and discriminatory economic system?

It should be observed that the church can very effectively be made the tool and creature of the surrounding economic culture by the collection-plate economy. The church's entry into the market place could make it less dependent on the whims of reactionary members. Furthermore, the most effective witness can often be made by entering into the economic activities of a given culture. Witness the Basel Mission Trading Company, which set the tone for European traders on the west coast of Africa in the nineteenth century.

Asian churches regard it highly desirable to get a piece of the action in their societies. The developing projects I witnessed in Asia were nearly all carried out without any help from abroad. But I was troubled to see some churchmen forced to pay interest rates as high as 30 per cent. Today Asian churches may need development capital perhaps even more than mission gifts. Uppsala's emphasis on Western Christian help for economic development is commendable. And the commercial project in Korea launched by the Emerging Economies Corporation under A. Eugene Adams and backed by church capital deserves wide support. But unless appropriate development loans are made to the churches in Asia, the gap between weak churches and increasingly dynamic economies will only widen. And the well-meant but one-sided help of Western Christians will only contribute to the growing frustration of Asian churches set in a context of dynamic social challenge.

WI JO KANG is Assistant Professor of History of Religions and Missions at Concordia Seminary. He received his B.D. degree from Concordia Seminary, and his M.A. and Ph.D. in history from the University of Chicago. Both his master's and doctor's dissertations were written under the direction of Professor Beaver. He taught in the religion department of Columbia University from 1964 to 1966, and at Valparaiso University from 1966 to 1968. He has published scholarly articles in the *Review of Religious Research*, the *Concordia Historical Institute Quarterly*, and the *Concordia Theological Monthly*. Under the auspices of the National Council of Churches in the U.S.A., he is now preparing with Professor Beaver a history of the Christian Church in Korea.

12

Wi Jo Kang: A Tribute to a Teacher

In East Asia there is a saying that a student shrinks even from stepping on the shadow of his teacher. This is a good indication of the reverence in which teachers are held there. But students from East Asia who have studied in the United States have said that while there may be many scholars in American universities, there are few outstanding educators. Too often, they say, American university professors are too impersonal, too busy, or too concerned for their own advancement to worry about the academic and personal concerns of their students. Nevertheless, some foreign students and many Americans are in fact fortunate enough to find eminent scholars who are at the same time able educators. R. Pierce Beaver is such a man.

Dr. Beaver is a professor at the Divinity School of the University of Chicago, and chairman of its church history field. His office is on the fourth floor of Swift Hall, in the center of the University campus. The Divinity School is not only older than the university itself, but is the heart of some of the most exciting intellectual activities on campus. In Dr. Beaver's office countless students from all over the world — not only from the University of Chicago, but from many other institutions as well — have been counseled and guided through successful academic careers. On June 30, 1971, Professor Beaver is retiring after a distinguished career.

Robert Pierce Beaver was born in Hamilton, Ohio, on May 26, 1906, the son of James Earl and Caroline Nuesch Beaver. In the summer of 1927, at the age of twenty-one, he married Wilma Manessier. They had two sons and a daughter. The daughter, Helen Barbara, is deceased. The elder son, David Pierce, is a professor at Moorehead State University, Moorehead, Kentucky. The younger son, Stephen Robert, is a foreign student advisor at the University of Toledo in Ohio.

Dr. Beaver received his early education in the town of his birth, graduating from Hamilton High School in 1924. At Oberlin College he gained his bachelor's degree, and in 1928 a master's degree in art. He did graduate work in history at Cornell University, where he earned his Ph.D. in 1933. Besides such degree programs, Pierce Beaver studied at the University of Munich from 1931 to 1932, and also at Yale University, the College of Chinese Studies in Peking, Union Theological Seminary, and Columbia University.

Professor Beaver came to the University of Chicago with experience in a rich variety of ministries. In 1932 he was ordained in the Reformed Church in the United States, now affiliated with the United Church of Christ. During the next four years he was a pastor in Cincinnati, and then from 1936 to 1938 he served congregations in Baltimore, Maryland. But of greatest import for his future career were the years from 1938 to 1947, spent as part of the China Mission of the Evangelical and Reformed Church. In fact he is presently a consultant to the Division of Overseas Ministries of the National Council of Churches of Christ, as well as to many mission boards, and he belongs to the Chicago Metropolitan Association of the United Churches of Christ. He participated in the Willingen and Ghana meetings of the International Missionary Council and in various World Council of Churches study consultations, such as those at Davos and Herrenalb, and in the Faith and Order study commissions on tradition and traditions.

As an academician he is a member of Phi Beta Kappa; Phi Kappa Phi; the American Society of Church History; the Society for the Scientific Study of Religion; the North American Academy of Ecumenists; the American Historical Association; the American Theological Library Association; the Association of Professors of Mission, of which he was a founder and president; and the Midwest Fellowship of Professors of Missions, which he also founded. Beaver is widely known in European academic circles and is a member of the Deutsche Gesellschaft für Missionswissenschaft. As a recognized scholar, he is listed in the *Authors' and Writers' Who's Who* (London) and in *Who's Who in America; Dictionary of American Scholars.* At present he is editing the "Christian World Mission Books," a series of mission studies published by the William B. Eerdmans Publishing Company in Grand Rapids, Michigan. He is also on the editorial board of *Church History* and the *Journal of Church and State.*

As an educator, Dr. Beaver has had a variety of experiences. At Cornell he was a graduate teaching assistant in ancient history from 1928 to 1930, and an instructor from 1930 to 1931. From 1940 to 1942, during his years in Asia, he served as professor of church history and worship at the Central China Union Theological Seminary. This was interrupted by internment under the Japanese in Hong Kong. Later he became professor of missions and ecumenics at Lancaster Theological Seminary, Lancaster, Pennsylvania. From 1948 to 1955, just prior to his coming to Chicago, Dr. Beaver was director of the Missionary Research Library, and research secretary for the Foreign Missions Conference of North America, which later became a division of the National Council of Churches in the U.S.A.

Dr. John Bennett, president of Union Theological Seminary, wrote in regard to Dr. Beaver's service at the Missionary Research Library: "He was an extraordinary librarian, or rather, strategist in building a library. His scholarship was very remarkable in its breadth, and in the tenacity of his hold on facts." And he was an "imaginative and devoted worker. He made of the library not merely a collection of books and materials, but a center of research. . . ."

While Professor Beaver was serving as director of the MRL, he also lectured at Union Theological Seminary, taught at Drew Theological Seminary (1950-51), and served as a part-time Professor of Missions at Biblical Seminary (now New York Theological Seminary). With his busy schedule of part-time lecturing in various schools, and his main responsibility at the Missionary Research Library, he was unable to devote his time to serious research, writing, or full-time teaching; much of his talent and scholarship went untapped. Since professors of missions were so rare, and since there was such a need for scholarship in the area, it would have been unfortunate indeed had

Professor Beaver continued his career at the library in New York. His scholarship and his teaching were sorely needed.

In 1953 two very young scholars in what was then known at Chicago as the Federated Theological Faculty, Professor Joseph Kitagawa, originally from Japan, at Chicago since 1950, and Dr. Jerald Brauer, who had joined the faculty in 1951, proposed that the University appoint a scholar in the area of Christian mission. The faculty agreed, recognizing the need for mission offerings in the theological curriculum. Since two-thirds of the world is non-Western, and since this non-Western world demands the Christian's concern and attention, theological education could not limit itself to traditional European religious thought or it would become provincial. Theological education must earnestly attempt to understand the whole contemporary world, and to relate the meaning of Christianity to that environment. Missiology could help to meet these demands.

Thus Professors Kitagawa and Brauer looked around for a specialist in the field. Both became convinced that the best man in the United States at the time was Dr. R. Pierce Beaver, who had already written a number of impressive articles in the professional journals. With the prodding of these two men, the Federated Theological Faculty considered Dr. Beaver. And they liked what they saw. Recognizing his ability and the great scholarly contributions he had already made, along with the varied missionary experience he had gained in China and in world travel, they offered him a full professorship. Professor Beaver accepted and in 1955 moved from New York to begin his new work.

In April of that year Jerald Brauer was appointed dean of the Divinity School. As dean he worked very closely with the newly appointed professor of mission, and many new and exciting programs emerged. About Professor Beaver's early days at Chicago Dean Brauer wrote to me: "He interjected into the life of the community a whole new worldwide outlook which, though not totally absent in the past, had no focus either in terms of person or of the curriculum through which its full effects might be made known." Professor Beaver began to develop a program for the Center for the Study of the Christian World Mission, which he still serves as director. The Center sponsored some important seminars and lectures, including an outstanding meeting in March of 1959. Its theme was "Christian Responsibility in the Emerging World Economic Situation." Demographer Philip Hauser presented a paper on the population explosion, and Professor Gibson Winter discussed what industrialization does to people. Other scholars presented papers on the effects of industrialization in specific parts of the world — in Latin America, Asia, and Africa. The members of the seminar, which included many mission-board officials, drafted a statement entitled, "The Responsibility of the Mission Boards and Young Churches."

The year after Professor Beaver joined the faculty at Chicago, another important event took place there. Professor Mircea Eliade, Rumanian diplomat and great scholar in the history of religions — called by Thomas Altizer the "shaman" of our time — also joined the faculty. Suddenly the University had the constellation of Eliade and Kitagawa in the history of religions, and Pierce Beaver in the history of missions and Christianity. Under the deanship of Jerald Brauer, these three outstanding scholars had by 1957 articulated an elaborate program for inter-cultural, inter-religious exchange between Buddhism in Southeast Asia and the Federated Theological Faculty. This program was supported for a time by a generous grant from the Rockefeller Foundation, enabling the University to exchange professors and students. Thus a new stage was reached in the life of the theological faculty at the University of Chicago: Chicago became a center for mission studies and research, and Professor Beaver was drawing outstanding missiologists both from this country and from all parts of the world. He was also attracting students, not only from the Divinity School, but from many departments of the University, especially the department of history.

Attending Professor Beaver's class was a remarkable experience. Members generally included missionaries and church leaders from every continent. Professor Beaver usually presented highly organized materials in series of lectures. Of course, there were frequently important discussions; but the material Professor Beaver presented in his lectures was so valuable that students wasted little time in pointless discussion, lest important subject matter be missed. If Dr. Beaver was unable to meet his students during the regular class hour, he would invite them to dinner in the evening, and afterwards would present his lecture. Mrs. Beaver was always an excellent cook, pleasing the tastes of Americans and foreigners alike, and was a kind and gracious hostess.

Nor was Professor Beaver's influence over his students limited to his courses. At his home there were monthly meetings of the "World Church Fellowship," an organization of students interested in mission studies. Usually, outstanding missionaries and theologians were invited to speak, and discussion followed. One of the most memorable meetings I can recall featured a presentation by Professor Joseph Sittler. The noted theologian at the University of Chicago had presented a major paper to the New Delhi assembly of the World Council of Churches. Upon his return to Chicago he was invited to Professor Beaver's home to report what he thought of the assembly. In this kind of informal meeting, students sat shoulder to shoulder in the Professor's living room with such noted teachers and churchmen as Bishop Anders Nygren, exchanging views with them.

As a scholar and educator, Professor Beaver took what was in many ways a strict, cautious, and firm approach to his students. Every paper would be carefully read, and extensive notes would be made in the margin. Some students disliked his caution in dealing with their dissertations and papers. They resented the time it consumed. But most appreciated his care. Dr. Beaver wanted his students' papers to meet high standards, to be worthy of respect in all academic communities.

Although Professor Beaver could draw on a rich background, he did not rely solely on past experience and training for his teaching material. In spite of his busy teaching and speaking schedule, he frequently took time to travel throughout the world. In doing so, he kept abreast of the rapidly changing scene in Christian missions, and he constantly conducted research to find new material. A number of significant articles in scholarly journals resulted. Traveling scholars are sometimes looked at askance in academic circles. But Dean Brauer appreciated Professor Beaver's taking time to explore the many new challenges on the front lines of the Christian encounter. Of the value of such travel the Dean wrote to me:

> First, due to his travels and lectures throughout the younger churches, the name of the Divinity School of the Uni-

versity of Chicago was once again familiar to all those churches. For a long time this dimension of the work of the school had been lost, in spite of the fact that Chicago had sent a large number of people, particularly in educational work, into the mission field. A second consequence was a steady output of scholarly books and monographs which both pinpointed the historical development of the Christian mission and highlighted the new situation in which the churches were called to live and work. Third, Professor Beaver proceeded to educate in a very disciplined and scholarly fashion a number of young scholars in the field of the history of missions.

In his travels Professor Beaver did not simply visit mission stations and church leaders and spend leisure hours observing foreign customs. His itinerary often included teaching assignments. In 1964, on one of his several trips to West Africa, he taught in the department of religious studies at the University of Ghana. Together with this kind of visiting relationship and travel, he maintained his membership on the governing committee of the African and American Universities' Exchange Program during the half-dozen years of its existence. With his extensive knowledge of Africa, Professor Beaver is a valuable member of the committee on African Studies at the University of Chicago.

But Professor Beaver's first love is in Asia. From 1938 to 1947 he was a missionary and teacher of theology in China. In 1956, '57, '59, '65, and '69-70 Professor Beaver traveled in South Asia, where in 1957 he presented the Carey lectures and delivered the convocation address at Serampore University. He also delivered the Barrow lectures in Taiwan in 1956 and 1957. He is a member of the Board of Trustees of the Foundation for Theological Education in Southeast Asia (formerly the board of founders of Nanking Theological Seminary), and has been chairman of its policy committee since 1961. He is also leader of the Institute for Teachers of Church History, Missions, History of Religions, and Ecumenics, of the Association of Theological Schools for Southeast Asia. Since 1968 he has been honorary president of the Southeast Asia Society of Church History and Ecumenics. In 1970 he delivered the Barrow Lectures, under the joint sponsorship of Academia Sinica, the National Taiwan

University, and Fu Jen Catholic University in Taiwan. He served for some years on the research committee of the International Missionary Council, and on the United Board of Christian Colleges in China, forerunner of the United Board for Christian Higher Education in Asia.

Professor Beaver has been a tireless researcher. On his journeys he never neglected his studies. Around Easter of 1968 he wrote to me from England, "I got my desired research done at the Church Missionary Society Archives and the library of Quaker House, and then spent the remaining days exploring the Korean Mission Archives in the Society for the Propagation of the Gospel." Of American church historians, especially as a missiologist, Professor Beaver is perhaps the most widely known scholar today in Europe, Africa, and Asia, especially in East Asia.

But his greatest contribution was made at the University of Chicago. Dean Brauer writes once again, "Within the brief period of fifteen years at the University of Chicago he revolutionized the teaching of the history of missions." Thus, as a churchman, as a scholar, and above all as an educator who has influenced and inspired many young students who came to learn under him, Professor Beaver's contribution has been enormous. We are deeply in his debt.

As Professor Beaver retires in 1971, Chicago will sorely miss him, and the academic world will miss him. But the contribution he has made will endure, both in his own scholarly achievements and in the tradition he leaves to his students. Indeed, while this festschrift is a warm expression of gratitude, a recognition of his greatness as scholar and educator, it is also an effort to continue in that tradition.

The Published Work of R. Pierce Beaver: Bibliography*

I. BOOKS

All Loves Excelling: American Protestant Women in World Mission. Grand Rapids: Eerdmans, 1968.

Below the Great Wall. Philadelphia: Christian Education Press, 1946.

The Christian World Mission: A Recommendation. Calcutta: Baptist Mission Press, 1957. (William Carey Memorial Lecture, Serampore College.)

Church, State and the American Indians. St. Louis: Concordia, 1966.

Ecumenical Beginnings in Protestant World Mission: A History of Comity. New York: Thomas Nelson & Sons, 1962.

Envoys of Peace. The Peace Witness in the Christian World Mission. Grand Rapids: Eerdmans, 1964.

From Missions to Mission. New York: Association Press, 1964.

The House of God. St. Louis: Eden, 1935.

The Missionary Between the Times. Garden City: Doubleday, 1968.

Pioneers in Mission. Grand Rapids: Eerdmans, 1966.

To Advance the Gospel: Selections from the Writings of Rufus Anderson. Grand Rapids: Eerdmans, 1967.

ed., *Christianity and African Education.* Grand Rapids: Eerdmans, 1966.

II. PAMPHLETS, SURVEYS, REPORTS

"The Christian World Mission on New Frontiers," *Covenant Quarterly,* November, 1956, whole number. (Nyval Lectures.)

Foreign Mission Agencies in the United States. New York: Missionary Research Library, 1953.

The North American Churches and the World Mission. New York: Committee on Research in Foreign Missions, Division of Foreign Missions, National Council of Churches, 1952.

Retirement Provisions for National Church Workers. A Survey of Mission Board Policy. New York: Committee on Research, Division of Foreign Missions, National Council of Churches.

Schools Attended by the Children of American Missionaries. New York: Missionary Research Library, 1954.

Theological Education in the Younger Churches, A Review of the Literature. New York: Missionary Research Library, 1953.

Towards a More Effective Ministry through Missionary Institutions. New

---

* Book Review articles not included.

York: Division of Foreign Missions, National Council of Churches, 1953.

III. ARTICLES IN SYMPOSIA

"Der Anteil Nordamerikas," *Weltmission in Ökumenischer Zeit,* ed. Gerhard Brenneke. Stuttgart: Evang. Missionsverlag, 1961.

"The Apostolate of the Church," *The Theology of the Christian World Mission,* ed. Gerald H. Anderson. New York: McGraw-Hill, 1961.

"Eschatology in American Missions," *Basileia. Walter Freytag zum 60. Geburtstag,* ed. Jan Hermelink and H. J. Margull. Stuttgart: Evang. Missionsverlag, 1959.

"Missionary Motivation through Three Centuries," *Reinterpretation in American Church History,* ed. Jerald C. Brauer, vol. V, *Essays in Divinity.* Chicago: University of Chicago Press, 1968.

"Rufus Anderson's Missionary Principles," *Christusprediking.* Studiën op het Terrein van de Zendingswetenschap Gewijd aan de Nagedachtenis van Professor Dr. Johan Herman Bavinck, ed. J. Van den Berg et al. Kampen: J. H. Kok N.V., 1965.

IV. OTHER ARTICLES

"American Missionary Efforts to Influence Government Indian Policy," *A Journal of Church and State,* V, 1 (May, 1963), pp. 77-94.

"American Missionary Methods in the Indian Missions of the 17th and 18th Centuries," *Journal of Presbyterian History,* June 1969.

"American Missionary Motivation before the Revolution," *Church History,* XXI, 2 (June, 1962).

"Answers to Critics of Asia and Africa," *World Encounter,* III, 5 (June, 1966), pp. 24-25. Reprinted in *Leader,* Nov., 1966, pp. 17-18.

"Are Lutherans Intransigent?" *World Encounter,* II, 5 (June, 1965), pp. 11-13.

"Die Aufgaben des heutigen Missionsdenkens," *Allgemeine Missions-Nachrichten.* Jahrg. 35, No. 4 (Aug., 1955), pp. 28-29.

"Augustine of Hippo, *Servus Servorum Christi,*" *Church History,* III, 3 (Sept., 1934), pp. 187-206.

"Building a Basic Missions Collection in a Theological Seminary Library," in
a. Summary of Proceedings, 9th Annual Conference, American Theological Library Association, 1955, App. D.;
b. Missionary Research Library *Occasional Bulletin,* VI, 5 (June 20, 1955).

"Centers of Vitality in Contemporary Hinduism," Missionary Research Library *Occasional Bulletin,* IX, 5 (May 27, 1958).

"Chondogyo and Korea," *The Journal of Bible and Religion,* XXX, 2 (April, 1962), pp. 115-122.

"Christian Ashrams in India," *Christian Century,* July 14, 1965.

"Christian Art in the Younger Churches, a Bibliography," M.R.L. *Occasional Bulletin,* III, 13 (Dec. 9, 1952).

"The Christian Faith and Other Religions: The Present Phase," *Proceed-*

THE PUBLISHED WORK OF R. PIERCE BEAVER: BIBLIOGRAPHY

ings of the Association of Professors of Missions, 3rd Biennial Meeting, 1956, pp. 57-72.

"Christian Missions in Indo-China," in M.R.L. Occasional Bulletin, IV, 15 (Dec. 23, 1953).

"Christian Theological Education in China," privately distributed by the Board of Founders of Nanking Theological Seminary, 1943.

"The Church: One, Holy, Catholic, and Apostolic," The Builder, X, 9 (Sept., 1947), pp. 12-13, 21, 23.

"Church, State and the Indians: Indian Missions in the New Nation," A Journal of Church and State, IV, 1 (May, 1962), pp. 11-30.

"The Churches and President Grant's Peace Policy," A Journal of Church and State, IV, 2 (Nov., 1962), pp. 174-190.

"The Concert of Prayer for Missions," Ecumenical Review, X, 4 (July, 1958), pp. 420-27.

"Distribution of the American Protestant Foreign Missionary Force in 1952," M.R.L. Occasional Bulletin, IV, 10 (July 13, 1953).

"Doctrina y Practica del 'Real Sacerdocio,'" La Nueva Democracia, July, 1954, pp. 44-47.

"The Donatist Circumcellions," Church History, IV, 2 (June, 1935), pp. 123-133.

"The Expansion of American Foreign Missionary Activities since 1945," M.R.L. Occasional Bulletin, V, 7 (June 4, 1954).

"Five Years of Literature on Protestant Missions," Church History, XXIV, 4 (Dec., 1956), pp. 366-371.

"The Genevan Mission to Brazil," The Reformed Journal, XVII, 6 (July-Aug., 1967).

"Historical Aspects of Church Relationships in the Near East," News Bulletin of the Near East Christian Council, July, 1954, pp. 5-9.

"International, Interdenominational, Interracial Teams. A Proposal for a Demonstration of Mission Unity," International Review of Missions, XLII, 168 (Oct., 1953), pp. 404-412.

"International, Interdenominational, Interracial Teams. A Proposal for a Demonstration of Mission Unity," prepared for the Executive Board Meeting, Division of Foreign Missions, NCCCUSA, March 9-10, 1955. Mimeographed. (Second half different than in the foregoing.)

"An Inventory of Current Research in Missions in the United States and Canada," Church History, XXII, 1 (March, 1953). Publ. also as a reprint.

"Is There a Revival of Buddhism?" M.R.L. Occasional Bulletin, V, 1 (Jan. 18, 1954).

"Jesuit Missions Through the Eighteenth Century," Church History, XXII, 4 (Dec., 1953). Publ. also as a reprint.

"Joseph Hough, an Early Miami Merchant," Ohio Archaeological and Historical Quarterly, XLV, 1 (Jan., 1936), pp. 37-45.

"Laymen, the Minute Men of the New Missionary Advance," New York, Division of Foreign Missions, National Council of Churches, 1954. Mimeographed.

"The Mau Mau Movement in Kenya, A Review Article," M.R.L. Occasional Bulletin, IV, 2 (Feb. 6, 1953). Also in Voice of Missions, March, 1953, pp. 8-9.

"The Miami Purchase of John Cleves Symmes," *Ohio Archaeological and Historical Quarterly*, XL, 2 (April, 1931), pp. 284-342.
"The Ministry of Reconciliation," *United Church Herald*, II, 4 (Feb. 12, 1959), pp. 7, 30.
"Missions and the New Nationalism" in
a. M.R.L. *Occasional Bulletin*, XII, 1 (Jan. 15, 1961);
b. *A Journal of Church and State*, III, 2 (Nov., 1961), pp. 149-171.
"Misjonsforsknings-biblioteket i New York," *Norsk Tidsskrift for Misjon*, Arg. VII, 2 (1953), pp. 107-113.
"The Missionary Research Library," M.R.L. *Occasional Bulletin*, VI, 9 (Dec. 6, 1955).
"The Missionary Research Library, A Sketch of Its History," *Occasional Bulletin*, XIX, 2 (Feb., 1968).
"Missionsundervisning och missionsforskning i Nordamerika," *Svensk Missions tidskrift* (1953), Häfte 3, pp. 173-180.
"Mutual Understanding and Study among Religions from the Viewpoint of the Christian Mission," *Bulletin of the Ramakrishna Mission Institute of Culture* (Calcutta), VIII, 10 (Oct., 1957), pp. 225-233.
"Nationalism and Missions," *Church History*, XXVI, 1 (March, 1957).
"New Patterns in Missions," *Lutheran Foreign Missions Conference of North America*, 43rd Annual Meeting, 1962.
"A New Program in the Study of the Christian World Mission," *Divinity School News* (Nov. 1, 1956), pp. 9-18.
"New Strategy for the New Day," *World Encounter*, I, 4 (April, 1964), pp. 8-11.
"North American Thought on the Fundamental Principles of Missions During the Twentieth Century," *Church History*, XXI, 4 (Dec., 1952). Publ. also as a reprint.
"Nytt liv i Buddhismen?" *Norsk Tidsskrift for Misjon*, Arg. VIII, 2, 1954, pp. 92-105.
"An Ohio Farmer in Middle Tennessee in 1865," *Tennessee Historical Magazine*, ser. II, vol. I, no. 1 (October, 1930), pp. 29-39.
"The Peace Witness in The Christian Mission," *Mennonite Quarterly*, XXXVIII, 2 (April, 1963), pp. 96-112.
"Pioneer Single Women Missionaries," Missionary Research Library *Occasional Bulletin*, IV, 12 (Sept. 30, 1953).
"The Protestant Foreign Missionary Enterprise of the United States," M.R.L. *Occasional Bulletin*, IV, 7 (May 8, 1953).
"The Organization of the Church of Africa," *Church History*, V, 2 (June, 1939), pp. 168-181.
"Race and Nationality in North American Foreign Missions," M.R.L. *Occasional Bulletin*, IV, 11 (August 14, 1953). Publ. also in *The Missionary Seer*, Dec., 1953, pp. 6-8.
"The Readiness of the World for the Mission," *Concordia Theological Monthly*, XXXIII, 1 (Jan., 1962), pp. 13-23.
"Recent Literature on Overseas Missionary Movements from 1300 to 1800," *Cahiers d'Histoire mondiale* (Paris), I, 1 (July, 1953), pp. 139-163. Published also as a reprint.
"The Religious Library and the Professor's Attitude," *Special Libraries*, February, 1949, pp. 57-61.

"A Report on the Reallocation of China Missionaries and Funds by North American Mission Boards," M.R.L. *Occasional Bulletin,* III, 14 (Dec. 24, 1952), pp. 1-6.

"Research and Some Recent Publications in the History of Missions," *Church History,* XX, 3 (Sept., 1951), pp. 85-90.

"The Resurgence of Religious Dialogue: The Way of Encounter," *Encounter,* XXV, 3 (Summer, 1964), pp. 335-351.

"Revolution in Missions? Some Comments on Current Trends," M.R.L. *Occasional Bulletin,* VI, 3 (April 12, 1955).

"The Rise of Denominational Empires," *World Encounter,* II, 5 (June, 1965), pp. 7-10.

"The Rise of Monasticism in the Church of Africa," *Church History,* VI, 4 (Dec., 1937), pp. 350-372.

"The Search for New Patterns of Christian Witness," *World Encounter,* II, 3 (Feb., 1965), pp. 8-12.

"Servants of Christ and Stewards of the Mysteries of God," *South India Churchman,* March, 1957, p. 36 (address delivered at the 1957 Convocation of Serampore College). Also in *United Theological College Magazine,* XXIII (June, 1957), pp. 810-834.

"Some Aspects of the Asian Situation and Their Significance for Training for the Service of the Church," *Concordia Theological Monthly,* XXVIII, 11 (Nov., 1957), pp. 810-834.

"Some Background Information for the Study Conference on Missionary Institutions," Buck Hill Falls, Pa., Dec. 8-9, 1953 (by R. Pierce Beaver and Constant H. Jacquet, Jr.). Mimeographed.

"Survey of Recent Theological Literature; Missions and Ecumenics," *Union Seminary Quarterly Review,* May, 1954, pp. 25-29.

"Sources of Current Information about Foreign Missions," M.R.L. *Occasional Bulletin,* IV, 1 (Jan. 21, 1953), pp. 1-6.

"Tools for the Study and Teaching of Missions," a paper read at the 1st meeting of the Assoc. of Professors of Missions, Southern Baptist Theol. Seminary, Louisville, Ky., June 12-13, 1952.

"Two Years of the Literature of Missions; a Review of the Period from the Spring of 1952 to the Spring of 1954," prepared for the 2nd annual meeting of the Assoc. of Professors of Missions, Chicago, June, 1954. Mimeographed.

"Unpleasant Realities: A Note on the Union Negro Troops at Fort Blakely," *Tennessee Historical Magazine,* ser. II, vol. 1, no. 2 (Jan., 1931), pp. 148-149.

"What Is an Indigenous Church?" *World Encounter,* II, 1 (Oct., 1964), pp. 6-11.

"Where Are the China Missionaries? A North American Report," *World Dominion and the World Today,* March-April, 1953, pp. 88-92.

"Who Is a Missionary?" *World Encounter,* III, 1 (Oct., 1965), pp. 14-17. Reprinted in *Leader,* Church of the Brethren, Feb., 1966, pp. 2-8.

"Why Ram Christianity Down Their Throats?" *World Encounter,* III, 2 (Dec., 1965), pp. 10-13.

"World Mission; A Reconciling Fellowship," *Chicago Theological Seminary Register,* Nov., 1955, pp. 4-11. Reprinted by Division of Foreign Missions.

V. ENCYCLOPEDIA AND YEARBOOK ARTICLES

Encyclopedia Britannica, various, especially "Missions."
Die Religion in Geschichte und Gegenwart, eleven articles on missions.
World Book (Junior Encyclopedia), various.
World Scope Encyclopedia Yearbook, annual article on "Religion" in 1953,
'54, '55, '56, '57, '58.
Notable American Women, 1607-1950, six biographical articles.
Westminster Dictionary of Church History, sixty articles.
Concise International Dictionary of Missions (ed. by Stephen Neill), thirty-
five articles.

VI. IN PREPARATION

A reader in the history of missions, for Doubleday and Company.
A study of Hannah Kilham, pioneer Quaker educator in West Africa.
The History of Christianity in Korea, with Professor Wi Jo Kang; for the
Asia Department of the Division of Overseas Ministries of the National
Council of Churches of Christ in the U.S.A.

MESSAGES OF APPRECIATION

My first contact with Dr. Pierce Beaver came when he was in charge of the Missionary Research Library in New York. I still have a vivid memory of our first meeting, and of an instant awareness that here was a man with an enthusiasm for research, and with an immense width of sympathy. Over the years I have marvelled at his grip on the great principles of Mission, his understanding of the problems facing Missions today, and his power of interpretative scholarship which illuminates the past and sheds light on the present.

To Advance the Gospel, *his study of* Rufus Anderson, *and* Pioneers in Mission *demonstrated his insight into history.* Church, State, and the American Indians *proved his ability to interpret a particular problem.* The Missionary Between the Times *showed how alive he has been to our world of upheaval.*

These are but one man's choice of a few of Dr. Beaver's writings which have been found most valuable. But books and articles are not the whole of any man's contribution. The generosity of his friendship, and the rich experience which can be distilled best in conversation, these are what I continue to value most.

Max Warren,
Sub-Dean of Westminster Abbey,
and, from 1942-1963, General
Secretary of the Church Missionary
Society of England

Pierce Beaver was Director of the Missionary Research Library when I first met him. I am one of the many throughout the world who have benefitted greatly by his bibliographical expertise in the field of Missions and associated subjects. The immense service he gave us through the Book Notes, Selected Bibliographies, Occasional Bulletins, etc., was very helpful. To him, the library was no ivory tower, however. His work has always remained closely related to the deepest concerns of the mission of the church. He traveled widely and shared what he had seen and experienced. He would even include such exotic places as Sweden in his travels. As Library Director and later as Professor he visited Uppsala on many memorable occasions. His lectures here, as elsewhere, opened wide horizons and gave new perspectives.

His books, including that splendid study Ecumenical Beginnings, *are admirable expressions of the immense vitality of American scholarship and research.*

It has been my privilege to enjoy Pierce Beaver's generous friendship throughout the years and Wilma and Pierce Beaver's hospitality at Sherman, Connecticut. I know that I am greatly enriched and inspired, strengthened and blessed by this fellowship.

Bengt Sundkler
Swedish Institute of Missionary
Research
Uppsala, Sweden

All those who labor in the field of missiology (whether in connection with the problems of contemporary missions or the history of past missions) are much indebted to the work of Pierce Beaver. I first became aware of the contribution he was making when he served as librarian of the Missionary Research Library in New York. He made that venerable institution throb with new life. Great quantities of new materials were added to its collection. He was especially farsighted in bringing in materials dealing with the nondenominational missions, which had been underestimated until that time and whose growing importance he was able to recognize.

After Dr. Beaver moved to the University of Chicago, he utilized the broad resources of that university for the study of questions relating to missions. His writings during the Chicago years have constituted an increasing stream of valuable works. Dr. Beaver has also marshalled and edited a variety of works by contemporary scholars, as in the series of Christian World Mission Books.

It is hard to realize that in addition to this academic activity Dr. Beaver has been constantly involved in the Christian world mission itself, practicing as well as teaching in his field. His wide travels and visits to mission projects for agencies such as the Foundation for Theological Education in Southeast Asia have done much to improve the quality of service rendered by missions today.

Those who are so indebted to him can only hope that their debt will increase in the years to come.

Charles W. Forman
Professor of Missions
The Divinity School
Yale University